OECD INSIGHTS

International
Migration

The human face of globalisation

Brian Keeley

ORGANISATION FOR ECONOMIC CO-OPERATION AND DEVELOPMENT

The OECD is a unique forum where the governments of 30 democracies work together to address the economic, social and environmental challenges of globalisation. The OECD is also at the forefront of efforts to understand and to help governments respond to new developments and concerns, such as corporate governance, the information economy and the challenges of an ageing population. The Organisation provides a setting where governments can compare policy experiences, seek answers to common problems, identify good practice and work to co-ordinate domestic and international policies.

The OECD member countries are: Australia, Austria, Belgium, Canada, the Czech Republic, Denmark, Finland, France, Germany, Greece, Hungary, Iceland, Ireland, Italy, Japan, Korea, Luxembourg, Mexico, the Netherlands, New Zealand, Norway, Poland, Portugal, the Slovak Republic, Spain, Sweden, Switzerland, Turkey, the United Kingdom and the United States. The Commission of the European Communities takes part in the work of the OECD.

OECD Publishing disseminates widely the results of the Organisation's statistics gathering and research on economic, social and environmental issues, as well as the conventions, guidelines and standards agreed by its members.

This work is published on the responsibility of the Secretary-General of the OECD. The opinions expressed and arguments employed herein do not necessarily reflect the official views of the Organisation or of the governments of its member countries.

Also available in French under the title:
Les essentiels de l'OCDE
Les migrations internationales

Foreword

Few phenomena have shaped human history as decisively as migration. Its influence is evident in our vibrant, multi-ethnic societies – ever-present reminders of the power of the human urge to seek a better life elsewhere. Immigration brings new ideas, new energy, new connections that are reflected in our daily lives in thousands of ways – we eat Italian pizzas, Indian curries and Japanese sushi, we shop in late-night corner stores run by hard-working immigrants, and many of us work for or interact daily with businesses created by migrants of great vision and energy.

But migration brings challenges, too. In many societies, not all newcomers have managed to integrate successfully. Children may struggle in school, parents may not find work or may do jobs that do not make best use of their skills, and whole families and communities may live on the edge of the social mainstream. With recession gripping on the world economy, these problems are likely only to grow. Immigrants are at particular risk of losing their jobs during downturns and, even when economies do recover, their job prospects tend to be worse than those of natives.

For OECD members, these issues are of special concern. Net migration to OECD countries has tripled since the 1960s and – even with the economic slowdown – is likely to continue at a strong pace in the years to come. Indeed, as populations age in OECD countries in the coming decades, we are likely to call on migrants to play an even bigger role in our societies, although of course we cannot expect them to solve all the challenges we will face.

Challenges and benefits – migration brings them both. But we can only hope to minimise the former and maximise the latter if we adopt a coherent policy response. And we can only create that if we under-

3

stand the facts of migration – the reality rather than the rhetoric that all too often clouds debates on migration.

It is here that the OECD has a unique role to play. Our work on migration includes tracking migration movements and describing the size and characteristics of immigrant populations; examining how young immigrants are doing in education and investigating ways to ensure they make the most of their abilities; investigating the integration of immigrants in the workforce; and seeking to ensure that migration benefits both developed and developing countries.

This work forms the backbone of *OECD Insights: International Migration*, which, like the rest of this series, aims to generate informed debate on key issues facing our societies. The drama and distortions that surround discussions of migration (influenced in large part by the persistence of irregular immigration) make the need for rational dialogue on this issue especially pressing. Without such dialogue, our societies will fail to build support for comprehensive policies that make the best of international migration – for the migrants themselves, for the societies in which they come to live and for those they leave behind.

Anthony Gooch
Director, Public Affairs
and Communications Directorate

Acknowledgements

The author very gratefully acknowledges the advice and assistance of Marilyn Achiron, Nick Bray, Orsetta Causa, David Crane, Emmanuel Dalmenesche, Jeff Dayton-Johnson, Martine Durand, Francesca Froy, Jean-Pierre Garson, Georges Lemaître, Patrick Love, Annabelle Mourougane, Stephen Seawright, Claire Shewbridge and Miho Taguma. The author wishes to express special thanks to Olga Kamensky for additional research and writing and to Vincent Gallart and Carolina Sandrin for additional research.

OECD Insights is a series of primers commissioned by the OECD's Public Affairs and Communications Directorate. They draw on the Organisation's research and expertise to introduce and explain some of today's most pressing social and economic issues to non-specialist readers.

CONTENTS

Currency Note

Currency references are in US dollars unless otherwise indicated.

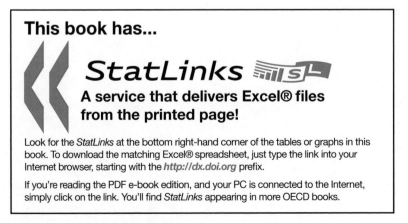

This book has...

StatLinks

A service that delivers Excel® files from the printed page!

Look for the *StatLinks* at the bottom right-hand corner of the tables or graphs in this book. To download the matching Excel® spreadsheet, just type the link into your Internet browser, starting with the *http://dx.doi.org* prefix.

If you're reading the PDF e-book edition, and your PC is connected to the Internet, simply click on the link. You'll find *StatLinks* appearing in more OECD books.

1

NO ENT

Few issues excite controversy like immigration, in part because it touches on so many other questions – economics, demographics, politics, national security, culture, language and even religion. That's why it's important to go beyond the rhetoric and get to the facts and realities of international migration.

The Migration Debate

By way of introduction...

It's easy to walk past the hostel in this unglamorous corner of Paris without noticing it. Open the doors and walk in, however, and the grey city street gives way to a very different world. This is Mali, or something close to it. In the hallways, men hang around in groups talking to each other. Some wear traditional boubou, or tunics, in deep blues and yellows; others wear cheap, faded denims and T-shirts. Almost all bear scars on their faces from tribal initiation rites.

Mali is present, too, in the meals these men eat, the scents of which drift up now and again from a kitchen in the basement, and in how this place is organised. Although these men are far from their home villages, they still respect their elders. As we sit talking with a group of men from the hostel, one of these elders comes in to find out what's going on. He is suspicious of visitors: the police have raided this place in the past and he doesn't want them back.

The legal status of the men who live here is not always clear. Some have French residency documents; others have not; some have permits that have expired; others have applications pending; one or two of the very few non-Malians who live here are applying for asylum. Among the men in the hostel, there are some who clearly don't want to attract the attention of the authorities. "I can return home, but there are others who can't because of their papers," says one man. "Like me", chimes in his neighbour, an older man in a tunic and with a salt-and-pepper beard. "It's been 17 years..."

Regardless of their status, the men want to work, and most do. Those who take too long to find work will eventually be asked to leave the hostel. One man explains that he was a builder back in Mali. When he came to France, he discovered that builders in Europe use cement, not the wood he was used to. "So now I am a cook," he says. "It's all a bit complicated, because I don't have my papers and so on. For all that, there is always work. But if I had my papers, I could do what I want to do. Because I want to make the most of my life, I am young."

Others are frustrated, too. "I have a salary. I can hit 1 300, even 1 400, even 1 600 euro a month," says one. "We're not asking for miracles. We just want a simple piece of paper... because to have rights here you must have your papers." They also want respect: "Some French people are afraid of those of us who live in these hostels. They think we're here to take their jobs, to injure them, that we're robbers, that we sell drugs... immigration is a stigma."

Yet, legal or not, and respected or not, the Malians will keep coming to France. Life is even tougher back in Africa. "The droughts are worsening," says one. "Before, two or three people could cultivate the land and feed ten. Today, all ten of those could work in the fields, and they wouldn't produce enough to feed even themselves."

In France, the Malians speak French, albeit not always fluently, and they have friends, and cousins, and brothers, and uncles here who can help them out as they settle in. They also know that, hard as things can be in France, they can help their families more by coming here than by staying in Mali. "We emigrate for our families, for our homes, for the people around us, for our village, not for our country," says one. "Apart from what I need to pay rent and to eat and for transport and for taxes, at the end of the month the rest is sent home to buy medicines, rice, [and] sugar."

The men, who come from just a few villages, have also pooled their money for collective projects back in Mali. "We are going to build small dispensaries to improve health – we've already built some," explains one of the men's leaders. "The government in Mali will find us doctors, and we will pay their salaries..."

Migration today... and tomorrow

The stories of these Malians are, of course, particular to them, but they also have echoes in the lives of millions of other immigrants and their families around the world. For immigrants everywhere, there are factors that push them to leave their homes and pull them to a new destination. There are webs of rules and regulations that determine legal status and who can go where. There are questions of language and work: can migrants speak enough of the local lingo to get by; are their skills relevant in their new country; and can they find a decent job. And there are the links with home, the sense of duty to support families left behind.

Today, around 2.9% of people on this planet – or around 190 million – are migrants, up from around 2.2% in the 1970. Although the number of migrants has generally been rising in absolute terms, this increase has been neither rapid nor consistent – the trend line has tended to move in fits and starts, rather than smoothly. Other than that, generalisations can be of doubtful value when talking about migration. Each migrant and each country experiences migration differently. Even within countries, there can be big variations between regions, and even between towns and villages, in the numbers who leave, and the numbers who arrive. Migration is thus both a global and, at times, very local phenomenon.

Age of mobility

Migration has always been part of the human story, and it will remain so. In future, more and more people in both developing and developed countries are likely to consider migrating, either permanently or temporarily, to seek out new opportunities. Improvements in transport links around the world have made it easier to travel, while the Internet is an ever-expanding storehouse of information on job prospects and life in other countries. Indeed, Ban Ki-moon, Secretary-General of the United Nations, argues we are entering an age of mobility, "when people will cross borders in ever greater numbers in pursuit of opportunity and a better life. They have the potential to chip away at the vast inequalities that characterise our time, and accelerate progress throughout the developing world".

Migrants are also likely to find themselves ever more in demand. Developed countries, like those in the OECD area, are likely to go on turning to immigrants to provide skills and expertise in areas like high-technology. Immigrants like Intel's Andy Grove, Yahoo's Jerry Yang and Google's Sergey Brin have been key to the global success of California's Silicon Valley, and there will be increasing international competition for such talent in the years to come – not least from emerging economies like India and China.

Developed countries are already using immigrants to make up shortfalls in their own workforces – especially in areas like information technology, healthcare, catering and agriculture. Migrants fill for more than a third of low-skill jobs in the United States, a share that – as in many other OECD countries – has been rising since the mid-1990s. This growth has been fuelled in part by the fact that more and more local people are spending longer in education and becoming more highly qualified, and so are increasingly unwilling to take on unskilled work. It has also been fuelled by the fact that the average age of people in OECD countries is rising. As birth rates fall and people live longer, populations are ageing, so, in future, there will be fewer workers to support the populations of children and retirees in just about every developed country. Today in the United States, for example, there are about four people of working age for every retiree; by 2050, that ratio is forecast to fall to about two workers for every retiree. In Italy and Japan, the ratios will be closer to one to one. Migrants will continue to help to fill some of this gap.

Of course, immigrants grow old, too. Any country relying solely on migration as a quick fix for ageing societies, or to make up shortfalls in key areas like science and technology and healthcare, is likely to be disappointed. Societies will also have to pursue other policy options, such as raising retirement ages, getting more people into the workforce and improving the education and training of locals.

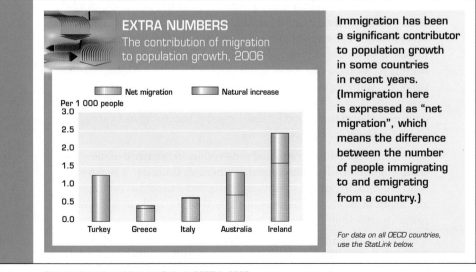

EXTRA NUMBERS

The contribution of migration to population growth, 2006

Immigration has been a significant contributor to population growth in some countries in recent years. (Immigration here is expressed as "net migration", which means the difference between the number of people immigrating to and emigrating from a country.)

Net migration   Natural increase

Per 1 000 people

For data on all OECD countries, use the StatLink below.

Source: International Migration Outlook: SOPEMI 2008.

StatLink : *http://dx.doi.org/10.1787/427158436323*

> **"To face the ageing challenge, increasing labour force participation is crucial. Immigrants can be part of the solution."**
>
> *Angel Gurría, OECD Secretary-General*
> *(speech in Lisbon, September 2007)*

Naturally, demand for migrants depends in part on the state of the economy, as does the willingness of people to leave their homes and try their chances in another country. As the financial crisis began to hit the global economy in 2008, there were already signs of a slowing down in immigration in some OECD countries such as the United States. As of now, it's too early to say how substantial that slowing is or how long it may last. But there is one thing that can be said for certain: even if flows of migrants slow, they won't stop. Migration will thus continue to be an important issue for governments, which will continue to face the challenge of designing policies that ensure that migration benefits migrants, the countries they go to and the countries they come from.

The migration debate

They will also have to deal with the reality that – like almost no other issue today – migration invites controversy. In part this is because it touches upon so many aspects of modern life – economics, demographics, politics, national security, social issues, national identity, culture, language and even religion. Opinion surveys show substantial antipathy to migration in many countries. In one poll for the *Financial Times* newspaper, just under half of Britons (47%) and a quarter of Spaniards (24%) said immigration from the rest of the euro area had been bad for their economy. In the United States, just over half of respondents (52%) believed immigration had done more harm than good for the economy, according to a survey for *The Wall Street Journal*/NBC News.

Such numbers don't give a real sense of the vehemence of views in what might be called "the migration debate". Consider a few recent contributions: in Europe, a politician calls undocumented immigrants an "army of evil"; on the message board of an Irish newspaper, a reader warns that "Irish people are slipping into a minority group within their own country"; in the United States, a TV anchorman warns that "the invasion of illegal aliens is threatening the health of many Americans", while a group advocating migration reform says "the country's ecology and resource base continue to be imperilled by mass immigration". And so on...

Such statements may be misguided, but they can't just be dismissed without some effort to try to understand what lies beneath. In many countries, concern about irregular and undocumented immigration is genuine, even if the nature of the phenomenon – especially the ways in which irregular immigrants enter countries – is not always well understood. There is also real concern about the integration of immigrants into mainstream societies. It's certainly true that in many countries, especially in Europe, some immigrant communities have been blighted by unemployment and low levels of educational achievement. Such problems can overshadow the success stories and contributions of many other immigrants.

What this book is about

What is the role of OECD in this debate? International migration was identified early on as a priority for the organisation, and it remains so today. All told, the 30 member countries of OECD welcome more immigrants than any other economic zone; in 2006, about 4 million immigrants settled permanently in OECD countries, about the same as in the previous year. Since the mid-1970s, the share of immigrants in the population of OECD countries has almost doubled to about 8.3%; by contrast, the share in less developed countries is much lower and, in some cases, has actually fallen. So, immigration is a major policy challenge in much of the OECD area. OECD works with member countries to find ways to meet these challenges, so that migration, whether temporary or permanent, is a positive for migrants, the societies they come to live in and the societies to which they move.

OECD's work on migration covers many different areas. It compiles data each year on the movement of migrants in the OECD area; it studies the impact of migration on economic growth; it examines the performance of migrants in education and employment, seeking ways to ensure that immigrants – and the societies they live in – can make the most of their talents and abilities; and it analyses the role of migration in developing countries, including the impact of the "brain drain" and remittances, or the money migrants send home to their families.

> **"The increasing role of migration in economic growth and development and the importance of international co-operation make the OECD a natural forum, and the best laboratory, for the analysis of the many facets of international migration."**
>
> *Angel Gurría, OECD Secretary-General*
> *(speech in Lisbon, September 2007)*

This book offers a brief introduction to some of this work. By necessity, it can provide only a limited overview of what is a now huge body of research and analysis by OECD on international migration. To give as full a sense as possible of this work, the book includes graphics and charts from a number of OECD publications and papers as well as direct quotations from their texts. At the end of each chapter, there's a section offering pointers to further information and reading from OECD, as well as links to other intergovernmental bodies and information sources on international migration.

Chapter 2 looks at the long history of human migration, and brings the story up to date by introducing OECD's data on who goes where today.

Chapter 3 examines the rules that govern international migration, and the ways that governments seek to manage the arrival of immigrants.

Chapter 4 looks at migrants and education – how well immigrants do in education, and what can be done to help raise low performances.

Chapter 5 focuses on migrants and work – the track record of immigrants in the job market, the barriers that holds them back and what can be done to lift them.

Chapter 6 looks at the role of migration in developing countries, including the impact of the "brain drain" and emigrants' remittances.

Finally, **Chapter 7** draws some conclusions on policy options for migration, and also looks at some key issues in the measurement of migration.

What is OECD?

The Organisation for Economic Co-operation and Development, or OECD, brings together the governments of countries committed to democracy and the market economy to tackle key economic, social and governance challenges in the globalised world economy. It has 30 member countries, the economies of which account for 68% of the world's trade and 78% of the world's Gross National Income, or GNI (a measure of countries' economic performance).

The OECD traces its roots back to the Marshall Plan that rebuilt Europe after World War II. The mission then was to work towards sustainable economic growth and employment and to raise people's living standards. These remain core goals of the OECD. The organisation also works to build sound economic growth, both for member countries and those in the developing world, and seeks to help the development of non-discriminatory global trade. With that in mind, the OECD has forged links with many of the world's emerging economies and shares expertise and exchanges views with more than 100 other countries and economies around the world.

In recent years, OECD has also begun a process of enlargement, inviting five other countries (Chile, Estonia, Israel, Russia and Slovenia) to open talks on joining the organisation, and offering enhanced engagement to five emerging economies (Brazil, China, India, Indonesia and South Africa).

Numbers are at the heart of the OECD's work. It is one of the world's leading sources for comparable data on subjects ranging from economic indicators to education and health. This data plays a key role in helping member governments to compare their policy experiences. The OECD also produces guidelines, recommendations and templates for international co-operation on areas such as taxation and technical issues that are essential for countries to make progress in the globalising economy.

www.oecd.org

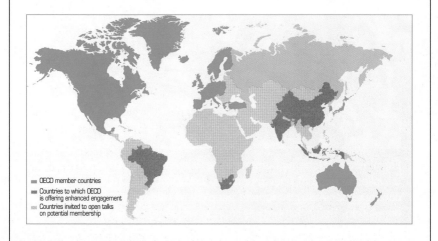

■ OECD member countries
■ Countries to which OECD is offering enhanced engagement
■ Countries invited to open talks on potential membership

2

For almost as long as humans have walked the Earth, they have travelled in hope of finding new and better homes. Today, that journey continues for many millions of people – all told, around 3% of the world's population. Remarkably, they experience many of the benefits, drawbacks and challenges that confronted earlier generations of migrants.

Migration
Then and Now

By way of introduction...

At a pier on the tip of Manhattan, the morning ferry is filling with tourists. They laugh and chat about the journey ahead, mostly in English but also in Chinese, French, Japanese, Filipino and many other languages. The ferry heads out into the Hudson river, leaving behind the skyscrapers of New York City, and then passes the Statue of Liberty, inscribed with the famous words, "Give me your tired, your poor, your huddled masses..."

A little later, the ferry docks at Ellis Island, where the tourists disembark and begin walking towards a great red-and-cream-coloured building, topped with four ornate towers, that looks like it might be some grand hotel in a European resort. But this was never a place to stay; it was a place to pass through, a transition point for new arrivals to the United States.

Over the course of many decades, around 12 million immigrants entered the US through here, beginning in 1892 with Annie Moore, a 15-year-old "rosy-cheeked Irish girl". Arriving within sight of New York, immigrants like Annie were herded into lines and marched into the main building on Ellis Island. There, in the space of about six seconds, health inspectors checked their condition. Any who appeared ill had letters chalked on to their clothes – "L" for lame, "Ct" for trachoma, "Pg" for pregnant – and were sent for further inspection.

Then, clutching their bags, the immigrants who made it through the health check walked upstairs to the Registry Room, where inspectors checked to ensure that they satisfied a few basic legal requirements, wouldn't become a burden on the public purse and could read 40 words in their own language. The exact requirements changed over the years, but even so most passed the tests; only around one in fifty were ever turned back.

Standing today under the vast, vaulted ceiling of the Registry Room, it's hard to imagine what it must have been like on 17 April 1907 – the busiest day ever on Ellis Island – when 11 747 people landed here. The room must have been filled with the smell of bodies unwashed after days and weeks on boats, and with the sound of thousands of voices speaking hundreds of languages, all talking about their hopes and fears for this new land...

▶ For a few decades around the turn of the 20th century, Ellis Island was at the centre of the long history of human migration until, once again, the story moved on. This chapter examines that history, from prehistoric times to our times, with the aim of showing, firstly, that the roots of present-day migration can often lie deep in the past and, secondly, that the patterns of the past are often repeated today. It concludes with a look at some explanations for why people migrate.

Migration yesterday

Migration is one of the great constants of human history – long before political border emerged, we were travelling the planet. Some of these journeys were cyclical, such as the seasonal treks of nomadic tribes with their grazing animals. Others were more open-ended – journeys begun in flight from natural disasters or in search of a better place to call home.

Scientists place the beginning of our global odyssey in eastern Africa and date it to around 50 000 or 60 000 years ago. Based on archaeological, genetic and linguistic evidence, it is believed that *homo sapiens'* first intercontinental move may have been into what we now call the Middle East, from where we moved into the Arabian Peninsula, around India and into southeast Asia and – probably – Australia. Later, we moved into southern and northern Europe and central Asia and then – *via* the Bering Strait – into North and South America.

Described like that in just a few sentences, it's easy to imagine this journey as a single, smooth and purposeful procession around the world. But, just as with migration today, there were no guarantees of success. Some groups thrived, others were wiped out by disease or conflict.

Throughout prehistory and into early recorded times, humanity's journey continued, both voluntarily and at the end of a sword – Greeks travelled and built cities and homes around the Mediterranean; Roman soldiers created an empire stretching from England to Turkey; the Mongols took China. Europe between the 4th and 7th centuries A.D. saw a period known as "the

2. Migration Then and Now

migration of the nations", when tribes like the Huns, Goths, Franks and Angles marched and sailed into new homelands, creating the foundations of today's European nation states.

Europe was at the heart of another great period of migration beginning around the 15th century and lasting for more than 300 years. The great routes developed by the European powers for trade were also conduits for human movements, both forced and voluntary. From Africa, millions of slaves were shipped in desperate conditions, often to work – and die – in the Americas and the Caribbean.

Later, as slavery was gradually abolished in Europe and the Americas, a steady flow of indentured labourers emerged to work in Europe's overseas plantations and in the Americas. These bonded labourers signed up – voluntarily or against their wills – for between five and seven years, usually with the promise of a return ticket home. Toiling for long hours and doing back-breaking work, their journeys took them around the world: Indians planted sugarcane in the Caribbean; Chinese "coolies" built railroads in East Africa;

What is migration?

Like any subject, international migration has its own terminology:

• **Emigration** refers to people leaving a country for long periods or permanently; **immigration** to people coming in; **international migration**, or, sometimes, just **migration** are catch-all terms covering both phenomena. **Permanent migration** means people intending to settle in another country "for good"; **temporary migration** covers people who intend to return home, often within a year, and who are usually travelling to work (sometimes **seasonally**, like fruit pickers) or for training or for a long working holiday.

• A migrant leaves an **origin** (or **sending**) **country** and goes to a **destination** (or **receiving**) **country**. Along the way, some, such as refugees and asylum seekers, may spend time in a **transit country**.

It's also common to hear countries spoken of in terms of whether they are **countries of emigration** (or sending or origin countries) or **countries of immigration** (or receiving or destination countries), even though these categorisations are not always clear cut. For instance, a country that is *mainly* experiencing emigration may also be experiencing some level of immigration. Nor are these terms permanent: economic or political change can see a country of emigration suddenly become a country of immigration, and *vice versa*.

• Finally, **net migration** represents the difference between levels of immigration and emigration: **negative net migration** means more people are leaving than arriving, and **positive net migration** means more are arriving.

22   OECD Insights: International Migration

and perhaps as many as a million Japanese went to work in the US, Hawaii, Peru and Brazil. At the end of their agreements many went back home, but many others stayed on. It may seem odd that people who had been through what were often brutal experiences would choose not to return home once their contracts ended. But one of the great lessons of migration throughout the ages is that things rarely work exactly to plan.

The European powers – the United Kingdom, Portugal, Spain, the Netherlands and others – sent their own people overseas, too. Spanish and Italians followed in the wake of Columbus to settlements in the Americas, while, later, more than a million Europeans would make their homes – at least for a while – in Algeria. But it was perhaps Britain that made the greatest use of such settlements – both forced and voluntary – to further its interests overseas. As early as 1606, a royal advisor told England's King James I that sending people overseas would serve "a double commodity, in the avoidance of people here, and in making use of them there". That advice was translated into action many times over the centuries: convicts were transported to Australia; orphans and children from troubled families were shipped off to Australia and North America; and Britons seeking a fresh start were sponsored to help settle "the colonies".

In the early years of the 19th century, another great period of migration began as a flood of Europeans – Russians, Italians, Irish and many more – sought to make a fresh start overseas. Over the course of more than a century, that tide would ebb and flow, but all told around 55 million Europeans are believed to have emigrated permanently in the century following 1820, mostly to North America and Australasia. Although migration was a different experience for each migrant and for each migrant group, there were broad themes in the story of transatlantic migration that were – and still are – common to people from many nations. Some of those themes can be glimpsed in the experiences of one of the largest groups of migrants, the Scandinavians.

Scandinavia was one of Europe's centres for migration, and initially most of those who left in the 19th century came from the countryside where "peace, the potato and the smallpox vaccine" had helped fuel a population boom. With land becoming tighter, rural Scandinavians had the choice of moving to cities in their own countries or going overseas. Many of those who left sought out the American Midwest, where they found land in abundance. Just as happens today, these emigrants encouraged their relatives and friends to follow them in waves of "chain migration". In the early 1870s, for instance, around two out of every five migrants leaving Oslo travelled on tickets sent by relatives. The influence of this phenomenon, where sisters followed brothers and nephews followed uncles to live in the same city or village, can still be seen in Midwestern states like Minnesota, where Scandinavian surnames like Johnson, Lindgren and Petersen abound.

Not only did migrants from various parts of Scandinavia tend to settle in the same areas, they also often worked to maintain their own identities – holding on to their native languages and religions for decades and rarely marrying outside their own communities. A letter from a Swedish immigrant in 1896 makes the point: "Many Swedes are settled here and more come each year, so there will soon be a little Sweden here, especially around the Swedish church. There is a post office and three stores as well as a Swedish doctor, Carlberg. The name of the place is Nya-Sverige, in English 'New Sweden'."

Other groups, too, like the Irish, Italians and Jews, only slowly integrated into the North American "melting pot," in part because they chose exclusion, in part because they were excluded. Today, integration remains one of the hottest issues in migration – should societies foster a spirit of multiculturalism, where migrants are encouraged to retain their own cultures and traditions, or should newcomers be expected to "blend in".

The scale of transatlantic migration in the 19th and early 20th centuries can obscure the fact that people were on the move in other parts of the world. In the 1850s, around 50 000 newcomers a year arrived in Australia, many drawn by the promise of gold. Chinese immigrants were the single largest group after Britons, but – as will be shown later – their welcome was not to last. The Chinese travelled elsewhere in the Asia-Pacific, too: between 1860 and 1915, around 3 million of them made new homes in southeast Asia, including in Thailand, Indonesia, present-day Malaysia and Singapore, the Philippines and India.

And, even within Europe's boundaries, there were extensive movements of people in the 19th and early 20th centuries. Britain saw an influx of Irish migrants after the potato famines of the 1840s. Later in the century, France witnessed a flood of Poles and Italians as the country's emerging industries struggled to find workers – a shortfall caused by falling birth rates in France and the reluctance of French smallholders to move to the cities. In 1881, there were around a million Italians in France; 50 years later their number had almost trebled to 2.7 million.

Passports, please

Looking back at the 19th and early 20th centuries, it can seem remarkable that migrants from much of the world – with a notable exception – travelled with very few restrictions. Providing they could afford their tickets and survived a possible health check on arrival, would-be emigrants normally needed no green cards or visas to make a fresh start in another country.

The exception was Asians. Starting in the 1850s in the Australian colonies, laws began to be passed in many of the major settlement countries to keep out Chinese, Indians, Japanese and other Asians. When federal Australia was established in 1901, one of its first acts was to institute a "white Australia policy", with one parliamentarian declaring that his countrymen were "determined that Australia shall be kept free from alien invasion and contamination". Australia was not alone. In the 1880s, Canada and the United States followed suit, effectively closing the door on Asian migrants. Gradually, over the next few decades, restrictions against migrants from other parts of the world began to pile up. In 1920, the United States finally ended its policy of free entry for Europeans and Latin Americans; in the 1930s, Canada began restricting immigration from southern and eastern Europe, favouring English-speaking migrants and dependents of existing residents.

These restrictions, fuelled by xenophobia and coupled with the great trauma of unprecedented global warfare and economic recession, sharply restricted voluntary migration across much of the world in the 1920s and 1930s. By the time it re-emerged in the mid-1940s – the beginning of the "thirty glorious years" of growth in North America, Europe and Japan – its character had changed.

Post-war migration

One of the major developments in migration in the post-war years was the emergence of the "guest worker". As western Europe rebuilt itself in the years after the war, countries like France, Belgium, Switzerland, the Netherlands and others actively

Who are the migrants?

The phrase "international migrants" covers a remarkably diverse group of people. Understanding this diversity can help explain why people migrate and provide clues to how countries can best manage the challenges and opportunities of migration.

Temporary labour migrants: Workers who travel for limited periods.

Long-term, low-skilled migrants: Receiving countries typically prefer these migrants to be temporary, but – as the experience of the guest workers in western Europe shows – this is often not the case.

Highly skilled and business migrants: Some transfer within multinationals while others are hired on the international job market. Recruitment of highly skilled migrants is becoming a major focus for some developed countries.

Irregular migrants: Also known as undocumented or illegal migrants. They are migrants who live in a country without the necessary documents. Some may arrive legally, but then overstay or work illegally. Migrant labour forces around the world include many irregular migrants.

Refugees: Defined by the United Nations as people living outside their own countries who are unable or unwilling to return home because of a "well-founded fear of persecution". Most OECD countries have given international commitments to shelter refugees. Although substantial in the past, refugee flows are not currently a major component of migration into the OECD area.

Asylum seekers: Definitions vary, but asylum seekers are mainly distinguished from refugees by the fact that they make their claim for protection as refugees when they arrive in the receiving country, and not in their own country or in an intermediate country. Governments frequently turn down asylum claims.

Forced migrants: May include refugees and asylum seekers, but also people fleeing famine and natural disasters.

Family members (family reunion and family formation): People joining relatives who are already living abroad as well as people who have married or are about to marry a resident of another country. The right to family reunion and to create a new family is widely recognised, including by Australia, Canada, the United States and most EU members, although rules vary considerably on who may be admitted.

Return migrants: People returning to their home countries after a period living abroad.

Source: Based on material in *Where Immigrant Students Succeed: A Comparative Review of Performance and Engagement in PISA 2003* (OECD, 2006), drawing from the work of Stephen Castles.

recruited workers from less economically advanced parts of the continent and further afield. Some came to do purely seasonal work, such as grape picking; others came on longer contracts to work in key industries, like car manufacturing.

No country was more associated with guest workers – or *gastarbeiter* – than the former Federal Republic of Germany (West Germany), where the number of foreign workers rose from 95 000 in 1956 to 2.6 million in 1973. The German experience with guest workers is a lesson in the law of unintended consequences. German politicians thought initially that they could hire mainly young men – and later young women – from countries such as Spain, Italy, Turkey, Yugoslavia and Morocco, who would work for short periods with no expectation of winning rights as citizens or being allowed to bring in families. But, as the Swiss writer Max Frisch famously said, "We wanted workers, we got people."

By the 1960s, Germany had no option but to relax its laws on family reunification as it competed with other European countries to hire overseas workers. As workers' ties with their home countries loosened, their economic roots in Germany deepened, although social integration and acceptance remained – and remains – elusive for many. The family of Eren Ünsal, a Berlin-based sociologist whose parents moved from Turkey in 1972, is typical of how time altered the plans both of politicians and migrants: "My mother insisted we were going to stay in Germany just long enough to earn money for a new sewing machine, to start a tailor shop back home," she told a reporter. "Now we're into the third generation, and my mother still hasn't bought her sewing machine. Of course, that's because they made comfortable lives. No one really wanted to go home."

Europe also looked for workers from its former empires and overseas territories. Fading since the 1920s, and even earlier, the old European empires all but vanished in the years following 1945. But old relationships remained. Many of the former European colonial powers saw arrivals from their former empires as they raced to rebuild their economies after the Second World War – Indians, Pakistanis and West Indians came to Britain; Moroccans, Tunisians and Senegalese to France; Surinamese and Indonesians to the Netherlands.

And permanent migration began again in some of the traditional settlement countries. Canada and Australia both encouraged mass immigration, gradually widening their scope beyond northern European countries, sometimes through the use of points systems. The United States, too, saw substantial numbers of new arrivals in the decades after the Second World War, albeit at only a fraction of the levels seen earlier in the 20th century.

The oil crash, and beyond

In the early 1970s, another turning point in the history of international migration: a global economic turndown triggered by the 1973 oil crisis effectively ended the mass recruitment of guest workers in Europe. Immigration stalled, but it didn't end. Far from it – in the decades following 1980, international migration took on new life: between 1985 and 1995, the numbers of migrants worldwide grew by 62% and more than doubled in the most developed nations.

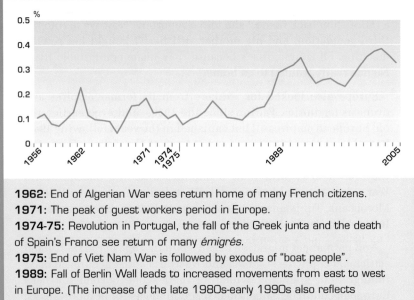

MOMENTS IN TIME
Net migration as a percentage of total population in OECD countries, 1956-2005

Net migration (immigration *minus* emigration) has been rising since the mid-1980s in OECD countries, albeit not smoothly. Indeed, as this chart shows, international migration tends to be marked by sudden peaks and troughs.

1962: End of Algerian War sees return home of many French citizens.
1971: The peak of guest workers period in Europe.
1974-75: Revolution in Portugal, the fall of the Greek junta and the death of Spain's Franco see return of many *émigrés*.
1975: End of Viet Nam War is followed by exodus of "boat people".
1989: Fall of Berlin Wall leads to increased movements from east to west in Europe. (The increase of the late 1980s-early 1990s also reflects a US decision to include irregular immigrants in its data.)

Source: *International Migration Outlook: SOPEMI 2007 (subsequently updated)*

StatLink ⫶⫶⫶ : *http://dx.doi.org/10.1787/015200172027*

> "Since about the oil crisis, the net migration rate within the OECD has been increasing, with international migration contributing more and more to population growth ..."
>
> *International Migration Outlook 2007*

The forces driving migration also evolved. Throughout the 1980s and into the 1990s economics became less important as a driver of immigration while other justifications – including family reunification and providing shelter to refugees and asylum-seekers – became more prominent. In the United States, migration rose significantly from the 1970s following a change in the law that made it easier for existing immigrants to bring in family members. This helped drive a shift in where migrants came from – Europe became less significant, and the Americas, especially Mexico and the rest of Latin America, as well as Asia became far more important. In the 1990s, the United States also started to provide new openings for migrants based on the skills they could bring to the economy – an approach that was also pursued in Australia and Canada.

In Europe, chain migration also became more noticeable, but there were other trends, too. Within the expanding European Union area, it became ever easier for EU citizens to go to work and live in other member countries, although relatively few chose to do so. More significantly, after the collapse of Iron Curtain in 1989, eastern Europeans were increasingly tempted to look west, a trend that accelerated in the early years of this century as the EU took in former Soviet-bloc countries like Lithuania, Poland and Hungary.

Migration today

So, what about migration today? The picture is, as it always has been, highly complex, but before looking at the details of who's going where, it's worth stepping back to note three major characteristics of migration in the early 21st century.

Firstly, migration is rising, and has been since the 1980s. The trend is neither steady nor consistent – for instance, the rate of increase slipped back in the 1990s. Still, the evidence is clear that migration is affecting ever greater numbers of people around the world. How

How migration varies across the OECD area

For a range of reasons – historical, cultural, economic and so on – each of the main migrant-receiving countries in the OECD area has attracted a different mix of immigrants. In some, permanent settlement has been the main theme; in others there have been influxes of short-term workers. Even still, the main immigration countries in the OECD area can be divided into four main categories:

1. The traditional settlement countries
Australia, Canada, New Zealand, the United States
These states were largely founded on immigration, and they continue to admit large numbers of immigrants for permanent residence.

2. European states that recruited labour in the post-war years ...
Austria, Germany, Luxembourg, Sweden, Switzerland
Many European states experienced substantial immigration (and, in some cases, emigration) over the course of their histories, but their development as modern nation states was not founded on it. Amid the labour shortages of the post-war years, these states – to a greater or lesser extent – actively recruited workers from abroad, often in the expectation that they would return home. However, many of these "guest workers" stayed on. Today, these states have quite high immigrant populations.

... some of which later shifted to humanitarian settlement
Sweden
Since the 1970s, Sweden and other Nordic countries like Denmark and Norway have placed a greater emphasis on admitting refugees and asylum seekers.

3. European states with migration linked to a colonial past and to post-war labour recruitment
Belgium, France, the Netherlands, the United Kingdom
The experience of these states has been reasonably similar to countries in the previous category (No. 2). However, for historical reasons, many immigrants to these states have tended to come from former colonies, and so are often able to speak the language of the country they settle in, which can have implications for social and educational integration.

4. New immigration countries
Ireland, Italy, Greece, Portugal, Spain, Denmark, Norway
A number of European states, previously countries largely of emigration, have in recent years become countries of immigration. As well as the arrival of foreign nationals, some of these states have also seen return emigration, most notably people who left as guest workers in the 1970s and 1980s.

And the rest... among other OECD countries, some, such as Japan, Korea and Finland, have low levels of immigration by international standards, while others, most notably Turkey and Mexico, are mainly countries of emigration.

many? The United Nations estimates that around 190 million – or a little under 3% – of the Earth's 6.7 billion people live outside their country of birth. That figure may seem low, but because migrants tend to move to a relatively small number of destinations, they may account for quite large slices of the population within individual countries. In the OECD area, migrants account for more than 23% of the population in both Australia and Switzerland but only around 3% in Finland and Hungary.

Secondly, migration is essentially a story of movements of people from poorer to richer – or, from less developed to more developed – countries. That characterisation can be a little deceptive, however. What it doesn't reveal is that there is also a very substantial amount of movement between developed countries (or, as they're sometimes collectively known, "the north") and between developing countries ("the south"). Overall, about one-third of the world's migrants travel from north to north, in other words from one developed country to another; another third travel from south to north; and the final third travel from south to south.

That said, there has been a clear shift in migration towards the world's most developed countries. In the mid-1970s, just under half of all migrants in the world lived in less developed countries, with 42% in more developed countries. Today, only a third of the world's migrants are in less developed countries, with 60% in more developed countries.

> "… if one plots the growth of immigration against other faucets of globalisation it is clearly a key component of the globalisation process".
>
> B. Lindsay Lionel, *Trends in International Migration Flows and Stocks, 1975-2005* (an OECD Working Paper)

Thirdly, international migration is part of an even larger social and economic process that has been helping to transform the world in recent decades – namely, globalisation. Just as goods and services are being traded more freely across borders, more and more people are looking to live and work overseas. And, although freedom of movement is not necessarily increasing – except within some economic zones like the European Union – there's increasing recognition of the role of migration as a component of globalisation and, at a national level, of the role of migrants in driving economic growth. In the years to come this is likely to translate into increasing competition, especially between developed countries, for highly skilled migrants.

Migration: some numbers...

This section introduces some basic numbers on migration in the OECD area.
By its nature, this data only covers legal and authorised migration, and not illegal and irregular migration, even though this is substantial in many countries.
Migration data makes a key distinction between "flows" and "stocks" of migrants:
• **Flows:** The number of migrants who have arrived in a country over a fixed period of time, such as the previous 12 months. "Net flows" refers to the number of people arriving into a country (immigrants) *minus* the number who are leaving (emigrants). A negative flow means more people are leaving than arriving, and a positive means more people are arriving.
• **Stocks:** The existing population of immigrants in a country (although, as Chapter 7 points out, countries take different approaches to how they count their immigrant populations).

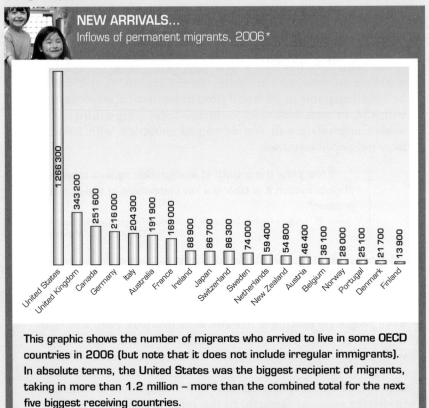

NEW ARRIVALS...
Inflows of permanent migrants, 2006*

This graphic shows the number of migrants who arrived to live in some OECD countries in 2006 (but note that it does not include irregular immigrants).
In absolute terms, the United States was the biggest recipient of migrants, taking in more than 1.2 million – more than the combined total for the next five biggest receiving countries.

* Data refers to permanent-type migration and reflects standardised statistics, which may differ from nationally published data.

Source: International Migration Outlook – SOPEMI 2008.
StatLink : http://dx.doi.org/10.1787/427003461010

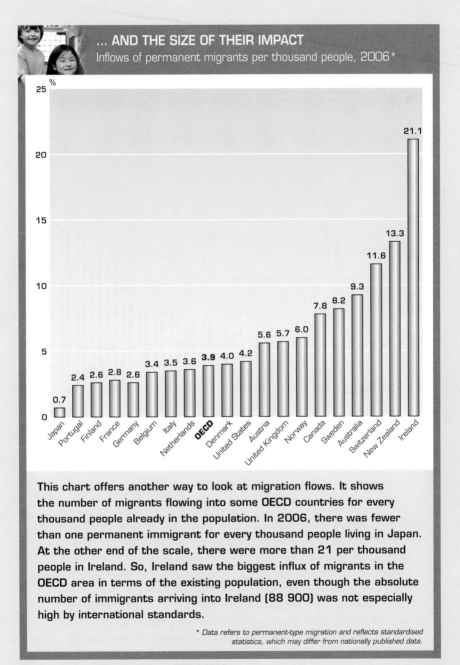

... AND THE SIZE OF THEIR IMPACT
Inflows of permanent migrants per thousand people, 2006*

This chart offers another way to look at migration flows. It shows the number of migrants flowing into some OECD countries for every thousand people already in the population. In 2006, there was fewer than one permanent immigrant for every thousand people living in Japan. At the other end of the scale, there were more than 21 per thousand people in Ireland. So, Ireland saw the biggest influx of migrants in the OECD area in terms of the existing population, even though the absolute number of immigrants arriving into Ireland (88 900) was not especially high by international standards.

* Data refers to permanent-type migration and reflects standardised statistics, which may differ from nationally published data.

Source: International Migration Outlook – SOPEMI 2008.
StatLink : http://dx.doi.org/10.1787/427133481271

2. Migration Then and Now

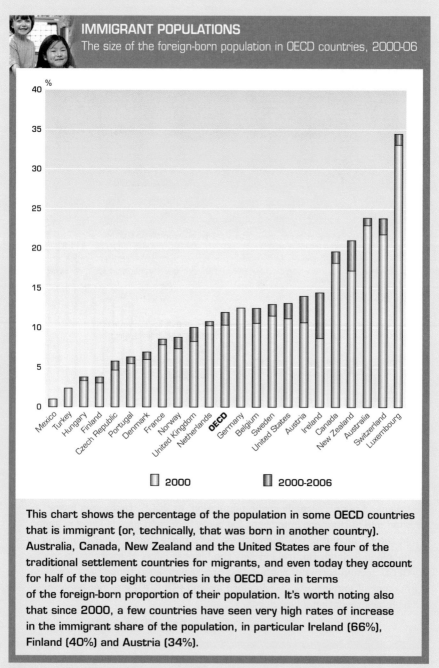

IMMIGRANT POPULATIONS
The size of the foreign-born population in OECD countries, 2000-06

☐ 2000   ☐ 2000-2006

This chart shows the percentage of the population in some **OECD** countries
that is immigrant (or, technically, that was born in another country).
Australia, Canada, New Zealand and the United States are four of the
traditional settlement countries for migrants, and even today they account
for half of the top eight countries in the **OECD** area in terms
of the foreign-born proportion of their population. It's worth noting also
that since 2000, a few countries have seen very high rates of increase
in the immigrant share of the population, in particular Ireland (66%),
Finland (40%) and Austria (34%).

Source: International Migration Outlook – SOPEMI 2008.

StatLink 🔗 : *http://dx.doi.org/10.1787/427243430285*

34   OECD Insights: International Migration

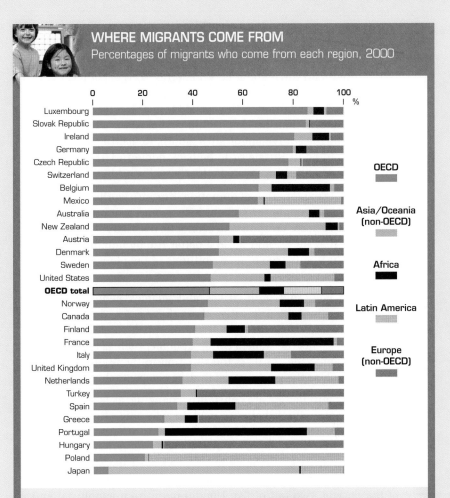

WHERE MIGRANTS COME FROM
Percentages of migrants who come from each region, 2000

Legend:
- OECD
- Asia/Oceania (non-OECD)
- Africa
- Latin America
- Europe (non-OECD)

Countries (top to bottom): Luxembourg, Slovak Republic, Ireland, Germany, Czech Republic, Switzerland, Belgium, Mexico, Australia, New Zealand, Austria, Denmark, Sweden, United States, **OECD total**, Norway, Canada, Finland, France, Italy, United Kingdom, Netherlands, Turkey, Spain, Greece, Portugal, Hungary, Poland, Japan

This chart shows where migrants came from in OECD countries in the year 2000 (the most recent year for which this sort of data is available). The numbers tells some interesting stories: for example, the colonial histories of Belgium, France and Portugal in Africa are reflected in the relatively high numbers of immigrants who come from Africa. Japanese migration, which is traditionally low, shows signs of two major influences: geographical proximity – most of its immigrants come from the Asia-Pacific region – and its history in the 19th and 20th centuries of sending workers to Latin America, the descendents of some of whom later returned to the land of their ancestors.

Source: OECD Factbook 2007.

StatLink ᵐᵖ : http://dx.doi.org/10.1787/516224313186

Why do people migrate?

In a provincial town about 60 kilometres northeast of Moscow, an Uzbek migrant is painting the pedestal of a bust of Lenin. It's not much of a job, but Kuram, a 49-year-old former tractor driver, says he's doing better than he was back in Uzbekistan, where he was only earning the equivalent of $16 a month. Reflecting on whether he'd prefer to be in Russia or to be back home in Uzbekistan, he tells a reporter, "If things were better there, I wouldn't be here."

As a simple explanation of migration, Kuram's words are hard to beat. For many people throughout history and around the world, migration has been a response to economic necessity – a reflection of the fact that they could build a better life by moving to a new country. But this is true of many billions of people, and yet most people don't migrate.

So what is it that both drives and enables people to move to another country? Typically, these forces are described by sociologists and economists in terms of "push" and "pull". The "push" represents the state of things at home, such as the strength of the economy; the "pull" is the situation in the migrant's target country, such as the prospects of finding a decent job.

Push and pull factors are constantly changing, as is the balance between them, which helps to explain why migration numbers fluctuate so much. An example: in the 1990s, the Central American country of Honduras saw increasing levels of emigration, a situation that was suddenly exacerbated in 1998 by Hurricane Mitch, which destroyed around 80% of the country's infrastructure. By the end of the decade, two out of five Hondurans were unemployed and three out of five were earning less than the official minimum wage of $128 a month. The push factors were clear, but there were also important pull factors, including the prospects of finding work in wealthier countries like the United States, and the existence there of well-established Honduran communities.

Those pull factors increased in the wake of Hurricane Mitch, in part because of a decision by the Honduran government to help its citizens to find work overseas, even if only for short periods. The government signed bilateral agreements that eased the way for Hondurans to take up seasonal jobs on Canadian farms and short-

PERSONAL VIEW — George Alagiah

George Alagiah is a journalist and anchorman with the BBC. In these reflections (edited for space), he reflects on his journey from Sri Lanka to London.

I was born in one continent, moved to a second and settled in a third. Asia, Africa and Europe; Sri Lanka, Ghana and Britain. They are stepping stones to a better life, landmarks along the journey of one migrant family.

Our motivation for leaving the land of our birth over 40 years ago was no different to the reason so many make similar journeys today. True, we took the legal route while some today opt for the sometimes perilous, often illegal and always expensive journey offered by the people smugglers. Yet others claim a sanctuary to which they are not entitled – they are economic migrants rather than people genuinely seeking refuge from persecution. But the impetus is the same as it was for us – a desire to improve on the poor hand dealt by fate.

The fact that these latter-day migrants are willing to risk so much underlines a fundamental truth about migration – the movement of people from poor and failing states to rich and stable ones is as inevitable as water running downhill. Every child who's ever built a sandbank on a beach will tell you just how futile it can be to try to stem the tide. If water is a force of nature, then migration is a force of history. The challenge is not to try to stop it but how to manage it. The first step is to see migration for what it is, rather than through the prejudiced eyes of some headline writers.

Historically, the net effect of migration has been a benign one. Where would America be without the unparalleled movement of Irish people in the mid-to-late 19th century? Where would modern Australia be if it had continued to rely solely on the flow of people from the "mother" country. And where would we, in Britain, be without the commercial energy and professional skills of the Indian diaspora?

When I discuss migration with people who have a rather different take on it there is always that comical moment when they realise that – despite my English tones – I am an immigrant. An embarrassed "oh but you are different" is the best they can offer to hide their prejudice. My answer is always the same. There is just as much chance that the timid Kosovan child who enrols in a school today will one day go on to read the news on the BBC.

I am where I am because I've been able to take advantage of the opportunities offered by a Britain at its best – a land of hope that is open and confident. To deny these chances to a new generation of migrants would be an injustice to the individuals concerned but, more important, it would mark a profound loss of faith in our nation's place in this new century of globalisation.

© BBC.

term contracts on ships run by lines in countries like Greece and the Netherlands. It also agreed an arrangement with the United States to regularise Honduran illegal immigrants and to let them stay there legally for 18 months.

The case of Honduras illustrates the point that migration never occurs in a vacuum. An individual's decision to stay or go is always shaped – and either facilitated or blocked – by a range of factors that go well beyond his or her own reach. Indeed, some analysts argue that the push-pull theory of migration places too much emphasis on the role of the individual's choice and ignores the wider social, economic, cultural and political contexts that may affect those choices.

To take account of all the wider forces that shape migrants' decisions, some sociologists prefer to think in terms of a more complex set of relationships described as "migration systems theory". This views migration as an interaction between, at one level, events and circumstances in the wider world and, at the other, the individual situation of the migrant. Or, to use the terminology, it represents the interaction between…

> Macro-structures: The economic and political state of nations and the world, globalisation, and laws and practices to control and manage migration. And

> Micro-structures: The migrant's own social networks of friends and family, community links to the destination country, the availability of information to migrants, and so on.

> A third level – meso-structure – is also sometimes identified, which covers the intermediaries in the migration process, including organisations that recruit migrants as well as agents and people smugglers.

Managing migration…

Journalist George Alagiah states in this chapter that "migration is a force of history". It is an illusion to think that it can be simply turned off. Migration has shaped our world and will continue to do so. Unquestionably, it brings challenges – for migrants, the countries they leave and those to which they travel. But it also has the potential to bring enormous rewards. As Alagiah says, the challenge is not to try to stop migration, "but how to manage it", and that is the theme of the next chapter.

Find Out More

On the Internet
For a general introduction to OECD work on international migration, visit *www.oecd.org/migration*.
For OECD statistics on international migration, go to *www.sourceoecd.org/database/oecdstat*. Click on *OECD.stat*; where there are two migration databases:
> International Migration Database contains OECD's most up-to-date data on international migration.
> Database on Immigrants in OECD Countries is based largely on data from the 2000 round of censuses in OECD countries.
OECD data can be also accessed *via www.oecd.org/statistics/demography*.

Publications
International Migration Outlook: SOPEMI: This annual Outlook provides the latest data on migration in the OECD area as well as assessments of the size of foreign and foreign-born populations and numbers of naturalisations. Notes on individual OECD member countries detail recent developments. Each edition also includes chapters devoted to topical issues in migration.

A Profile of Immigrant Populations in the 21st Century: Data from OECD Countries (2008): This book describes the origin and structural characteristics of immigrant populations in OECD countries. Nine thematic chapters cover issues including the age structures of immigrant populations, education and employment levels and migrants' occupations. Other issues covered include the gender dimension of the brain drain and the migration of health professionals.

Also of interest:
Trends in International Migration Flows and Stocks, B. Lindsay Lowell (2007): This OECD "working paper" discusses trends in

international migration over the past three decades and some of their demographic and policy implications.
www.oecd.org/els/workingpapers.

Migration and the Global Economy: Some Stylised Facts (2008): John P. Martin of the OECD discusses migration as part of globalisation and compares current and previous waves of international migration. *www.oecd.org/els/migration/policies*.

The International Organisation for Migration (*www.iom.int*): IOM is an intergovernmental organisation that promotes international co-operation on migration issues, seeks solutions to migration problems and provides humanitarian assistance to migrants.

United Nations Department of Economic and Social Affairs – Population Division (*www.un.org/esa/population/unpop.htm*): This UN division studies migration flows as part of its broader role to monitor and assess the impact of population changes. See also *http://esa.un.org/migration/*.

Global Commission on International Migration (*www.gcim.org*): Launched on the initiative of the United Nations and some member governments, the GCIM was asked "to provide the framework for the formulation of a coherent, comprehensive and global response to the issue of international migration". Its remit ended in 2005, when it published its final report.

Global Migration Group (*www.un.int/iom/GMG.html*): This group of intergovernmental agencies aims to promote "the wider application of all relevant international and regional instruments and norms relating to migration, and to encourage the adoption of more coherent, comprehensive and better coordinated approaches to the issue of international migration".

Managing Migration

Migrants who wish to travel legally are rarely free to go wherever they want. Their movements are governed by a raft of rules, conventions and regulations that determine who may go where. But, equally, international agreements can give migrants significant rights to settle.

By way of introduction...

The photo is grainy and coloured in the lurid grey-green of night-vision camera equipment. It shows two parallel wire fences, each perhaps more than three metres tall. The fence on the left is topped with coils of barbed wire. Standing against it are a number of rough ladders on which some men are climbing. A few have reached the top; more stand behind, waiting their turn.

Strange as it may seem, if the men make it across the second fence, they will have passed over one of the world's great frontiers – the border between Africa and Europe. The Mediterranean marks much of the boundary between these two continents but, thanks to the details of history, there still remain a few tiny outposts of European territory along the northern African coast. In 2005, two of these enclaves, the Spanish territories of Ceuta and Melilla, jumped into the news when five would-be African migrants were killed on just one day as they tried to climb the fences.

In recent years, increasing numbers of would-be migrants have tried to make their way in Ceuta and Melilla. One migrant told a reporter about his attempt: "Every night, people try to climb over the twin barbed wire fence... After two weeks, a Moroccan man showed us a tunnel which had been dug underneath the fence. We tried to get through, but when we were just 200 metres from the tunnel, we heard the sound of heavy boots running towards us – we had been sold out."

It's not surprising that images and reports of illegal migrants feature regularly in the media. These are dramatic stories filled with human interest, and they can also play to deep-seated fears of "invasion" by outsiders. Indeed, a glance at the headlines can give the impression that migration is basically chaotic and unregulated. The reality, however, is even more complex...

▶ Irregular migration forms only a part of the overall flow of migrants, but it attracts the lion's share of publicity. What this can obscure are the rules, conventions and regulations that govern migration, and which both empower – and sometimes limit – governments in determining who comes to live within national borders. This chapter looks at how these systems work, and at how governments manage migration.

Who can travel?

What right do we have to travel? Most – albeit not all – countries allow most of their adult citizens to leave and return without restriction. This right, known as freedom of movement, is enshrined in many national constitutions and in international law. As far back as 1215, the English charter of freedoms, Magna Carta, declared that "it shall be lawful to any person, for the future, to go out of our kingdom, and to return", while in the 20th century the Universal Declaration of Human Rights set down that "everyone has the right to leave any country, including his own, and to return to his country".

However, the freedom to leave one's country isn't usually matched by an equal freedom to enter another. Restrictions vary greatly: anyone wishing to set foot in Vatican City – a sovereign power – only has to continue walking down Via della Conciliazione in Rome and then step into St. Peter's Square; anyone wishing to enter Saudi Arabia or the Himalayan kingdom of Bhutan had better start thinking about visas well in advance. In short, while we're usually free to leave our own country, there are no international laws guaranteeing entry to all other countries.

> **"While migration is on the rise, there is no comprehensive international legal framework governing the cross border movement of people."**
>
> *Trade and Migration*

The freedom of countries to police their own borders – to decide on who and what may pass – is zealously guarded, and is often regarded as a defining feature of modern sovereignty. Citizens expect their governments to exercise this right, and failure, or even perceived failure, can come at a high political price.

Indeed, as election campaigns around the world have shown, controlling borders, and particularly migrant flows, is a hot issue. Take Switzerland, where a campaign poster created huge controversy in the 2007 general election with its depiction of white sheep kicking a black sheep off the Swiss flag. The poster was produced by a mainstream party, which said it was aimed at highlighting what it claimed were high crime rates among foreign nationals in Switzerland. But, in a country with one of the highest per capita migration rates in the world, many saw the poster as a veiled attack on all immigrants, while Switzerland's own president described it as "unacceptable". Elsewhere, a poll by the Pew Research Centre in 2007 found that people in all but two of 47 countries and territories surveyed around the world favoured tighter restrictions and controls on immigration (the exceptions were Korea and the Palestinian territories).

Irregular migration

Public antipathy to migrants is fuelled in part by the existence of irregular immigration, also referred to variously as "illegal", "undocumented" or "unauthorised" migration, and at times described in near apocalyptic terms by politicians and the media – words like "flood" and "deluge" are not uncommon. In reality, estimating numbers of irregular migrants is notoriously difficult, in large part because irregular migrants don't usually want to draw attention to themselves. Using different counting methods based on censuses or immigration forms or regularisations, it is possible to come up with estimates for some countries. At the low end of the scale are Japan and Australia, where irregular immigrants were estimated in 2005 to account for only about 0.2% of the population. Based on regularisations, the population in Spain was put at about 1.6% in 2005; in Greece it was put at about 3.4% after a 2001 regularisation. And based on census data, the population in the United States was put at about 4%, or 11.6 million, in 2006. Roughly speaking, then, in OECD countries that have reasonably high levels of immigration and which are not geographically cut off, between about 1% and 3% of the total population may be made up of irregular immigrants.

If working out accurate headcounts is difficult, so is defining what is meant by terms like "illegal" migration. For example, even though the media often features reports of immigrants climbing fences or landing on beaches, most irregular immigrants – especially in Europe – enter host countries legally, usually on student or tourist visas. It is only subsequently when travellers on such visas overstay or take up work that their position becomes irregular. Data for Italy suggest that just under two-thirds of irregular immigrants are overstayers, while even in the United States – which has long land borders with Mexico and Canada, and so plenty of potential entry points – it's estimated that about 45% of irregular immigrants still entered the country legally.

And even when immigrants are clearly irregular, governments or officials may effectively turn a blind eye. For more than three decades up to the mid-1980s, the "Texas Proviso" in US legislation essentially gave employers immunity from prosecution for hiring irregular immigrants, thus cutting off an important channel for targeting such immigration. The United States is certainly not alone in this. In countries around the world, there is a tendency to send mixed messages on irregular immigration. Officially, it may be condemned; unofficially, it may be tolerated.

Migrants may also find their status changing almost overnight. Italy, the United States, Greece, Portugal and others have all launched one-off mass amnesty programmes to let irregular migrants regularise their situation. Spain – once a country of emigration but now one mainly of immigration, especially for people from eastern Europe, South America and, increasingly, North Africa – has organised five "regularisation" or "normalisation" programmes in just 15 years. The most recent was in 2005 and attracted around 690 000 applications, around 40% of which were for Latin American immigrants. Unusually, the 2005 programme placed the onus for registration on the employers of irregular immigrants, which was in part a recognition of the importance of immigrants – legal and irregular – to the country's economy. Spain, like some other countries, also operates a "rolling amnesty" that allows irregular migrants to qualify for residency or the right to work after living in the country for a fixed period of time.

Such one-off regularisations, which are usually targeted at specific groups of immigrants, can serve as official recognition that bureaucracy or the law has failed to keep up with changing realities. For example, Belgium regularised asylum seekers who filed applications but who had received no reply from the government even after several years. Regularisations can also be inspired by that idea that irregular immigrants forge real and meaningful links in the societies in which they are living, and deserve to be given the legal and civic protections that other citizens enjoy.

> "Targeted regularisation concerns specific categories of foreigners. As a rule, they are cases where the authorities acknowledge the legitimacy of residence despite the lack of authorisation."
>
> *International Migration Outlook: SOPEMI 2007*

Against this complex and ambiguous background, many international agencies and governments prefer to use the term "irregular" rather than "illegal". This preference can also be driven by repugnance at the use of the word "illegal". As Lawrence Downes of *The New York Times* has written:

> Since the word modifies not the crime but the whole person, it goes too far. It spreads, like a stain that cannot wash out. It leaves its target diminished as a human, a lifetime member of a presumptive criminal class. People are often surprised to learn that illegal immigrants have rights. Really? Constitutional rights? But aren't they illegal? Of course they have rights: They have the presumption of innocence and the civil liberties that the Constitution wisely bestows on all people, not just citizens.

Irregular migrants often play a useful role in the economy, but their status means they may not always pay their full share of taxes and charges – a source of considerable resentment and a hot political issue in many countries. Irregular immigrants may also place themselves at considerable risk, sometimes paying for their journeys with their own lives. At the very least, they may have to pay large sums of money to people smugglers. According to estimates by *The Economist*, irregular migrants pay from about $1 000 for a journey from Mexico to Arizona in the United States to as much as $60 000 to go from China to the US.

Irregular migrants may also find themselves working as virtual slaves in their adopted countries, unable to seek help from officials for fear of expulsion. Indeed, many of the major benefits of irregular immigration come not to the immigrant but to the employer, who can usually get away with wages that are far below the local going rate and avoid paying welfare contributions. The immigrant, meanwhile, has minimal bargaining power, and may have to work excessive hours with no guarantee even of receiving wages. Indeed, employers play a role in effectively encouraging irregular immigration around the world. The willingness of some to hire people without confirming their status offers irregular migrants the possibility of finding work, and creates a powerful incentive for them to cross borders in the first place.

International agreements

Governments tackle irregular immigration in many ways – including monitoring borders and entry points, such as ports and airports, deportations, fining employers of undocumented migrants, and so on. Increasingly, many OECD members have sought to work

GLOBAL VIEW   What is Mode 4?

Since 2001, countries around the world have been holding on-off negotiations on a new global trade agreement, which – if it is finally agreed – could cover some very narrowly defined forms of temporary migration. Carried out under the auspices of the World Trade Organisation, the so-called Doha round of trade talks aims to rebalance world trade more towards the needs of developing countries. One element of the talks on this new agreement is focused on "GATS Mode 4", or "the movement of natural persons".

This needs a little explaining: "GATS" is the General Agreement on Trade and Services, a global agreement that was reached in the mid-1990s and which defined four ways, or "modes", through which services can be delivered internationally. (A quick reminder on goods and services: buy bread from a baker and you're buying a good; buy a haircut from a hairdresser and you're buying a service.) So, Mode 2 covers industries that cater for people who come from overseas to buy their services, for example tourism; Mode 3 covers companies that set up in another country to deliver services, for example an international chain of beauty salons.

Mode 4 covers people who sell their services in another country, for example a Dutch plumber who goes to fix a tap in Luxembourg, but not someone who goes to another country to become a salaried employee.

The key point about Mode 4 is that it covers only temporary movements, and only the movements of people selling a specific skill. The problem comes in defining temporary: is it a question of weeks or years? And what does it mean to sell a skill? Should that cover only the highly skilled, like a lawyers and accountants, or could it include people like fruit-pickers?

Developing and developed countries don't see eye to eye on many of these issues. For instance, many developing countries believe a comprehensive deal on Mode 4 could provide their people with lucrative opportunities overseas, and could help to provide a balance to the relative advantage that companies from developed countries enjoy when it comes to setting up overseas (Mode 3). By contrast, many developed countries believe that Mode 4 covers issues that go beyond trade to touch on areas like migration. They question whether an international trade agreement is really the place to deal with such issues.

Only time will tell how these questions are resolved. For now at least, it looks like most of these questions will continue to be dealt with through bilateral agreements or within economic zones like the European Union.

with the countries where irregular immigrants come from, in some cases signing agreements to clamp down on irregular immigrants in return for allowing more immigrants to land with full rights.

Such arrangements are part of a huge number of international bilateral agreements relating to various aspects of migration. Because migration is not governed by a single international treaty, there's a whole swathe of one-off government-to-government agreements – at the last count, OECD countries had signed at least 170 such pacts. That sounds like a lot, but most of them cover only seasonal, contract and guest workers or young people on working holidays, and the numbers of migrants involved are relatively low. There are also many agreements between non-OECD countries, such as the one that allows almost 150 000 Philippine domestic helpers to work in Hong Kong, China.

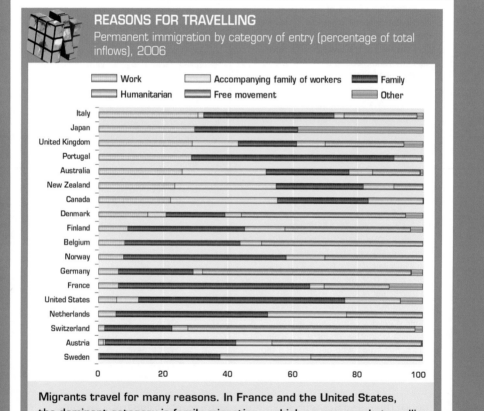

REASONS FOR TRAVELLING

Permanent immigration by category of entry (percentage of total inflows), 2006

Legend: Work | Accompanying family of workers | Family | Humanitarian | Free movement | Other

Countries (top to bottom): Italy, Japan, United Kingdom, Portugal, Australia, New Zealand, Canada, Denmark, Finland, Belgium, Norway, Germany, France, United States, Netherlands, Switzerland, Austria, Sweden

X-axis: 0, 20, 40, 60, 80, 100

Migrants travel for many reasons. In France and the United States, the dominant category is family migration – which covers people travelling to join relatives who are already settled in those countries or to marry existing residents. In Switzerland, most immigrants travel because they have a right to work and live in the country.

Source: *International Migration Outlook: SOPEMI 2008*.

StatLink ᴍᴬᴾ : *http://dx.doi.org/10.1787/427163172430*

Who has the right to enter?

Irregular migration forms only one side of the migration story. The other, and more substantial side, is authorised entry – immigrants who are allowed to enter countries for any number of reasons, such as to work and live permanently or temporarily, to accompany family members who are taking up jobs, to reunite with relatives who have been established for some time or to flee persecution. Most countries have immigrants who fall into just about all these, and even some other categories, such as cultural exchanges for artists and musicians and working-holiday schemes for young people.

However, certain categories of immigration tend to dominate in some countries. In the United States and France, family concerns are the main driver, including migrants bringing in family – both when they immigrate or subsequently – and people who are migrating to get married; in Sweden, humanitarian issues are dominant; in Australia, Canada and Switzerland, labour is the biggest category.

As the previous chapter discussed, there are other differences in the types of immigration experienced by various OECD countries. Canada, the United States, Australia and New Zealand have traditionally been known as "settlement countries". In effect, most of those who immigrate are seeking to settle permanently, and they – or a member of their family – have passed through some form of selection process. By contrast, in much of Europe, migration tends to happen within free-movement areas, and selection plays much less of a role. (As for the rest of the OECD area, Mexico is essentially a country of emigration, while both Korea and Japan have relatively low levels of immigration by international standards.)

But even where it may appear on the surface that countries operate highly selective migration policies, the reality is that most immigrants enter not because they have been specifically selected (either by government or an employer) but because they are entitled to do so. There are a number of reasons for this.

> **"... In all countries, there are significant immigration movements over which governments have limited discretion."**
>
> *International Migration Outlook: SOPEMI 2006*

Firstly, OECD countries now generally support the idea of family reunion as a basic human right, and most have signed up to international agreements that support this idea. The result is that if a husband or wife is living and working legally in an OECD country, there's a reasonably good chance that their spouse and children will be allowed to come and live with them. And although the rules vary greatly around the world, some countries also allow other family members, such as parents, to settle. Governments also tend to allow what's called "family formation", which can involve either local people or immigrants marrying foreigners, who are then given rights to settle.

Secondly, most OECD countries have signed up to international agreements covering refugees and asylum seekers, which means they commit to take in a certain number of people fleeing war, persecution or natural disasters. Establishing just who has a right to asylum or refugee status can be a contentious issue, however, and there are frequent complaints from international aid organisations that governments do not always live up to their commitments.

Finally, many OECD countries belong to free-movement areas – such as the European Union, the Nordic Passport Union, and the Australia-New Zealand Trans-Tasman Union – in which most citizens enjoy the right to cross borders to live and work in partner countries.

The result is that across the OECD area, most migration can be classed as "non-discretionary", in other words, immigrants have not been individually selected to enter either by governments or employers but are exercising a right to relocate, including within a free-movement area. By contrast, "discretionary" migration – in its narrowest sense – indicates that a migrant has been selected to enter.

A few numbers illustrate these points. Even the OECD countries that make greatest use of immigrant selection, such as Canada and Australia, directly select no more than one in four of all newcomers for work or settlement. In the United States, the number falls to just one in twenty. So who are the other immigrants? In many cases, they are the spouses and children of people who have been selected for entry. Where this is the case, they too are included in the category of "discretionary migration" because, it's argued, they typically share many of the characteristics of selected immigrants – such as wealth and current or future levels of education – even if they themselves haven't gone through the selection process. Working from this definition, between 60% and 70% of migrants to countries like

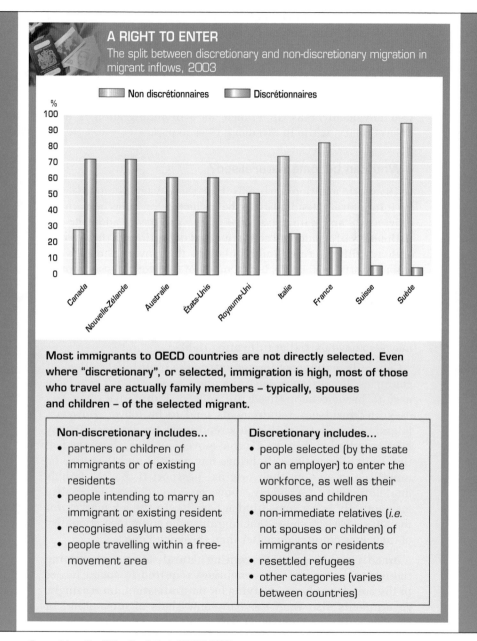

A RIGHT TO ENTER

The split between discretionary and non-discretionary migration in migrant inflows, 2003

Legend: ▨ Non discrétionnaires   ▨ Discrétionnaires

(y-axis: % 100, 90, 80, 70, 60, 50, 40, 30, 20, 10, 0)

(x-axis categories: Canada, Nouvelle-Zélande, Australie, États-Unis, Royaume-Uni, Italie, France, Suisse, Suède)

Most immigrants to OECD countries are not directly selected. Even where "discretionary", or selected, immigration is high, most of those who travel are actually family members – typically, spouses and children – of the selected migrant.

Non-discretionary includes...	Discretionary includes...
• partners or children of immigrants or of existing residents • people intending to marry an immigrant or existing resident • recognised asylum seekers • people travelling within a free-movement area	• people selected (by the state or an employer) to enter the workforce, as well as their spouses and children • non-immediate relatives (*i.e.* not spouses or children) of immigrants or residents • resettled refugees • other categories (varies between countries)

Source: International Migration Outlook: SOPEMI 2006.

StatLink ▦ : *http://dx.doi.org/10.1786/748054673522*

the United States, Canada and Australia can be said to fall into the category of discretionary migration.

With the exception of the United Kingdom, the situation in Europe's main countries of immigration is very different. There, most immigration is non-discretionary – it consists mainly of family reunion or of people travelling for work within free-movement areas. In France, 83% of immigration is non-discretionary, while in Sweden it rises to 95%.

Who can become naturalised?

It's worth mentioning briefly that these varying approaches to immigration tend also to be reflected in rules governing citizenship and naturalisation – or the process of adopting the nationality of an adopted country. Legal definitions of these terms – along with the rules and regulations that govern them – vary from country to country, but in much of the world these amount to pretty much the same thing: an immigrant who becomes a national gains the rights of a citizen, which translates mainly into the right to vote and to stand for elected office. (However, in some countries, permanent residents who are not naturalised may also have partial or full voting rights.)

Generally, permanent immigrants to the traditional settlement countries, for instance Australia and Canada, find it relatively easy to become naturalised. In much of Europe it's often less easy and residency requirements tend to be longer. However, migrants may not feel that this represents a major loss. If they have travelled within the EU free-movement area, they may feel that switching nationality brings few benefits and they may be unwilling to give up their original passport if the law forbids dual-nationality. Arguably, however, switching nationality may actually bring some hidden benefits. In the job market, for instance, research shows that migrants who adopt the nationality of their new country do better than those who don't.

Broadly speaking, rules governing naturalisation are becoming tighter, with migrants in some cases required to spend longer in the country before qualifying for naturalisation. Increasingly, governments also want them to show signs of integration. In Norway, future citizens must pass a test in Norwegian or Sami, the language of the indigenous people in the far north of Europe; in the Netherlands and the United Kingdom, naturalisation now involves a formal ceremony.

> **"The aim... is to verify the extent of foreigners' integration before granting them nationality, though the criteria on which verification is based vary considerably from one country to another."**
>
> *International Migration Outlook: SOPEMI 2007*

Naturalisation rules also vary when it comes to the children of immigrants. Broadly speaking, there are two main approaches, known by the Latin terms *jus soli* (right of the soil) and *jus sanguinis* (right of the blood). *Jus soli* effectively means that anybody born on a country's territory becomes a national of that country, regardless of their parents' nationality; by contrast, *jus sanguinis* means children acquire their parents' nationality (the lines can become blurred when it comes to children with parents who have more than one nationality or in situations where countries allow people to hold more than one nationality).

Are migration priorities shifting?

It hardly needs saying that there are considerable political pressures in many – if not most – countries to limit migration, and that politicians can find it hard to convince their publics of the case for bringing in outsiders. Such resistance is only likely to grow in the midst of an economic slowdown. Yet, there has been increasing awareness in many OECD countries in recent years that certain types of immigration may need to rise.

In part, this is a response to falling birth rates and ageing populations in developed countries, which, as *Chapter 1* mentioned, will dramatically increase the proportion of inactive elderly people in the years to come. So it's likely that developed countries will look to migrants both to supplement their workforces and to help care for the growing numbers of elderly people.

But a reminder: Immigrants grow older, too. The idea that societies can simply call on outsiders to "top up" their workforces and armies of carers without wider social and economic implications is simplistic. Yes, migrants will probably play a greater role in many developed economies, but there will also have to be other changes, such as getting more locally born people into the workforce, raising skill and educational levels – which helps lift productivity – and raising retirement ages.

> "... it is unrealistic to believe that immigration alone can offset future labour shortages, not to mention demographic decline. Furthermore, the very size of the flows would pose serious integration problems."
>
> *Martine Durand, Migration for Employment:*
> *Bilateral Agreements at a Crossroads*

There's also a realisation, particularly in Europe, of the role immigrants have played in high-tech industries in the United States. Jerry Yang, co-founder of Yahoo!, and who was born in Chinese Taipei, has said that "Yahoo would not be an American company today if the United States had not welcomed my family

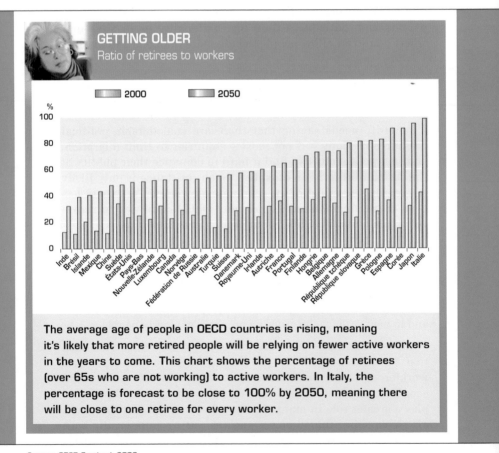

GETTING OLDER
Ratio of retirees to workers

The average age of people in **OECD** countries is rising, meaning it's likely that more retired people will be relying on fewer active workers in the years to come. This chart shows the percentage of retirees (over 65s who are not working) to active workers. In Italy, the percentage is forecast to be close to 100% by 2050, meaning there will be close to one retiree for every worker.

Source: OECD Factbook 2008.

StatLink : *http://dx.doi.org/10.1787/266404458420*

OECD Insights: International Migration

and me almost 30 years ago." Indeed, a study in the United States found that immigrants were key founders in just over half of Silicon Valley start-up companies, and were inventors or co-inventors in around a quarter of international patent applications filed from the United States in 2006. In the euro area, there tends to be fewer high-skilled migrants than in, say, Australia. In response, the European Commission has proposed a "blue card" programme for high-skilled migrants to mirror the United States' green card system.

Shifting priorities

Today, many OECD countries – particularly in Europe – are shifting their immigration policies. In part, these changes reflect new economic realities and the evolving role of migrants in labour markets. But, arguably, they are also due in part to increasing expressions of public concern over the presence of "outsiders" in their societies. To some extent, these are linked to perceptions of an increased security threat from the presence of immigrants. A number of commentators argue that events like the September 11 attacks in the United States in 2001, and the July 7 bombings in London in 2005, have led to an increasing "securitisation" of migration issues, with attempts to link immigration to terrorism and crime such as drug smuggling. There's also been increasing debate over how well migrants have integrated into societies. Incidents like the killing of the controversial Dutch director, Theo van Gogh, by a radical Islamist in 2004 have been used to highlight perceptions of "separateness" between some migrant groups and local populations. Antipathy towards migrants as a whole has also been fuelled by concern over the high rates of unemployment and weak educational performance prevalent in some migrant communities, including into the second and third generation, as well as by high-profile incidents that reflect upon the lives of a small minority of migrants, such as fake asylum claims. No doubt also, some politicians have sought to make political capital from these public concerns.

Whatever the reasons, there have been some steps in many OECD countries in recent years to make traditional migration more difficult, especially in the area of family migration. Germany, for instance, has made an initial move towards requiring family-reunification immigrants to take a language test before leaving home, while France now requires applicants to be resident for 18 months, rather than 12, before applying for the right to bring in family.

MIGRATION IN A RECESSION — Changing flows

Does immigration fall in recessions? Yes, although the impact varies between countries and among different groups of migrants. Labour migration – where people travel mainly to work – tends to fall most; family migration – where people travel to join relatives or to start a family – may not change that much.

A weaker 'pull'

There are two main reasons why net migration (immigration minus emigration) tends to fall as economies weaken. Firstly, the prospect of finding a job is an important "pull" factor for immigrants. If unemployment rises, that attraction is weakened. Secondly, people already living in the country may emigrate to look for work.

It will take some time before the full impact on migration of this recession becomes evident. As noted earlier, family migration is likely to be more resilient than labour migration. Because it accounts for a growing share of immigration into OECD countries, recessions are tending to have less of an impact on migration flows than in the past. Also, as family migration is more important in some places than in others, the slowdown in migration flows will vary between countries.

Close the doors?

During recessions, there can be pressure to "save jobs for locals". Even without such calls, governments may look for ways to reduce the numbers of people competing for scarce jobs.

For example, during the recessions of the 1970s, many European countries shut their doors to "guest workers". Already, there are some signs of shifts in migration policy. For example, some countries are issuing fewer temporary labour permits. There have also been cuts in permanent migration: In 2009, Australia cut its skilled migration programme by 14%. Countries have made other changes, such as reducing lists of occupations in short supply.

But there are limits on how much governments can do. Much immigration to the OECD area is "non-discretionary" – it involves migrants who essentially have a right to settle abroad, perhaps because they live in a free-movement area like the EU. There may also be limits on how much governments should do. Recession or not, there will remain a long-term need for imported labour in many OECD countries, in part because of ageing populations but also because of staff shortages in areas like health care.

Policy challenges

Governments thus face some tough challenges to design acceptable migration policies that respond adequately to the short-term economic shock without undermining long-term labour needs. Changes to policies in areas like family reunification must also be given careful thought, otherwise they may lead to immigrants bypassing legal routes, so increasing irregular immigration.

There is also a new emphasis on encouraging immigrants to play a bigger role in managing their own integration. Language courses are becoming widespread, as are information programmes that provide practical advice and describe the country's administrative systems and the formalities to be fulfilled. The flip side of such programmes is that migrants are increasingly likely to be asked to demonstrate that they have the knowledge and skills needed to navigate life in their new homes. So, for example, the United Kingdom has introduced basic language standards for immigrants seeking citizenship, and also requires them to pass the "Life in the UK" test, which covers everything from paying utility bills to the role of institutions like the monarchy and parliament and the names of British regional accents.

> "The rise of anti-immigration political parties and the perception that the integration of immigrants has not always been adequate have led in some countries to more restrictive policies with respect to family reunification..."
>
> *International Migration Outlook: SOPEMI 2006*

"Pro-active" policies

At the same time, there are some signs of a shift to so-called "pro-active" migration policies aimed at encouraging skilled migrants to fill particular gaps in the workforce, especially in areas like information technology, medicine, and bioengineering. In 2005, the United Nations asked governments around the world if they were planning to increase the number of highly skilled migrants that they admit. Fifteen of 46 more developed states said yes, they were (as did 14 of 98 less developed nations).

How is this translating into policy? At the very least, most countries have made their policies on labour migration more flexible, while others have launched specific recruitment programmes. There have also been moves, by countries like Norway and the United Kingdom, to relax laws that require even highly skilled migrants to have a job offer before they land; instead, they may be allowed to enter for a while to scout around for opportunities. Other countries are offering financial incentives to skilled migrants, which means they may enjoy virtual tax-free status for a number of years.

At the core of a pro-active approach is selection – allowing immigrants to enter because they have certain skills or abilities that may be in short supply in the receiving country. And in general, this selection is done in one of two ways, by the state or by employers.

Selection by employers

Employer selection is the norm in most of Europe, and it's aimed mainly at satisfying – sometimes short-term – gaps in the labour market, rather than adding to the population of permanent immigrants. One of its most obvious benefits is that there's usually a close link between the entry of migrants and the real needs of labour markets; it's unlikely, after all, that employers will bring in people for whom they have no work.

From the perspective of the state, employer selection also means immigrants are unlikely to impose a burden by requiring high levels of social support – at least not at first. But what if an immigrant subsequently loses his or her job? This can raise the risk of what's sometimes called "moral hazard" – an employer may gain all the benefits of bringing in an immigrant, but if things go wrong it is society, and not the employer, who must pay the costs.

From the perspective of the economy, a supply of well-qualified migrants can provide much-needed skills, and so keep down wage demands in sectors where labour supply is tight. But, according to economic theory, this may turn into a double-edged sword. Salaries are in part a reflection of supply and demand – put simply, higher salaries go to people whose skills are in greater demand. If a market is working efficiently, skills shortages will lead to higher demand and thus higher salaries, providing an incentive for workers to move into these areas. Arguably, this process of salary adjustment will slow if immigration is not restricted to areas of the economy where there are genuine skill shortages. (It should be noted, however, that a process like this takes time to play out. Also, markets rarely work completely efficiently: a higher salary is likely to be only one factor in attracting people to choose or change professions.)

One partial guard against this can be to insist on an "employment test", which requires employers to show that there is nobody locally who can do the job. In addition, the state can also set minimum skill requirements for immigrant workers, while still leaving it up to employers to make the actual selection.

> **"In many countries where unemployment rates are high, either nationally or among groups or regions, this test is rarely passed and few work permits are approved."**
> *International Migration Outlook: SOPEMI 2006*

There can be other downsides to employer selection, especially for the immigrants themselves. Migrants hired as temporary workers may find themselves contractually and legally bound to the hiring employer – in effect, they have a visa only for as long as their employer is willing to sponsor them. That can give an employer a powerful hold over migrant workers if they try to complain about working or living conditions. In some countries, such as in the Gulf region, the situation is worsened by the fact that labour laws may not cover migrants.

Even where laws treat both local and immigrant workers equally, migrants may be unaware of their rights and unwilling to risk losing their job. A migrant-rights group in Ireland reported on the case of trained chef from Pakistan who worked 18-hour days, seven days a week. As well as cooking, he was expected to wash up and clear tables and even deliver takeaway food. His salary was no more than half of what he had been promised, and even then a third of what he earned was taken away each week to pay for his work permit. Fear of deportation and a failure to understand his rights kept the chef from speaking out.

Selection by the state

State selection is the dominant method in the traditional countries of settlement – Australia, Canada, New Zealand and the United States – and its main aim is usually as a path to permanent settlement. Because of this, it's usually expected that migrants will bring in not just themselves but their families too, which can increase the long-term social costs on host countries. (That said, many employer-selected migrants will also bring in families.)

Would-be immigrants are usually screened for a qualities judged important for them to make an economic contribution, as well as to integrate into society. Typically, applicants are given points for certain characteristics, such as age, language ability, educational attainment, work experience, availability of funds, presence of family in the host country, having skills that are in short supply and – in some cases – having a job offer from an employer in the host country.

Most countries that use such systems set limits to the number of immigrants who can come in each year, and they may also shift the selection process to favour certain skills and characteristics. So, for instance, if doctors suddenly come into demand in a country that uses a points system to admit migrants, the points awarded to applicants for having a medical training might rise. In some countries, such as Australia and Canada, regional and local government may also play a role in selecting immigrants to match local labour-force needs.

Typically, the criticisms that are made of state-selection systems is that they can lack transparency – the processes by which immigrant target numbers are set are not always clear. Such systems may also move rather slowly, which can deter would-be applicants and delay responses to the emergence of skill gaps in the economy. Countries often ease these delays, however, with systems for temporary migration, which address short-term needs.

Skills and education

This chapter has spoken about how governments in OECD countries are becoming increasingly interested in encouraging skilled immigration. But even as that trend grows, it's easy to forget that education and skill levels among migrants are already quite high: On average, just over 23% of foreign-born people in OECD countries are university graduates, against about 19% of natives. That represents a very welcome "brain gain" for developed economies, but there's another, more worrying, side of the coin: Migrants are also over-represented among the less well educated, which raises concerns over their abilities to find long-term employment and make their own way in the world. The next chapter will look at migrants and education, examining how well they do in school and why, and what can be done to help them make up any shortfalls.

Find Out More

FROM OECD...

On the Internet
For an introduction to OECD work on managing migration flows, go to *www.oecd.org/migration*, and follow the link to "international migration policies".

Publications

International Migration Outlook: SOPEMI: This publication includes an annual update of recent developments in migration policy in OECD countries.

International Migration Outlook: SOPEMI – 2006 Edition: A special chapter, "Managing Migration – Are Quotas and Numerical Limits the Solution?", looks at the use of numerical limits to manage migration. As part of its coverage, it looks at how much control countries actually have over who can come to live in them, and also describes various methods for capping or targeting migration.

Migration for Employment: Bilateral Agreements at a Crossroads (2004): This report offers an overview of bilateral agreements and other forms of labour recruitment of foreigners in several OECD and non-OECD countries. It describes the management and implementation of these practices and analyses their impact on labour markets, economic development and migration policies of both sending and receiving countries. It also examines the prospects for this type of migration.

Trade and Migration: Building Bridges for Global Labour Mobility (2004): This book looks at some issues in the debate on trade and migration as they relate to international negotiations on trade in services and proposals for the freeing up the movement of service providers. It also explores ideas for building greater understanding between policy makers in the areas of trade and migration, and seeks ways to unleash the potential of the temporary movement of service suppliers to bring significant gains to both developed and developing countries.

... AND OTHER SOURCES

International Migration Law Database (*www.imldb.iom.int/section.do*): Operated by the International Migration Organisation, this database is a source for the "norms and instruments regulating migration at the international, regional and national levels".

United Nations High Commissioner for Human Rights (*www.ohchr.org*): UNHCR work includes the general protection of migrants' human rights and the protection of migrant workers and their families.

United Nations High Commissioner for Refugees (*www.unhcr.org*): The UNHCR is the UN agency for refugees. Although it is primarily concerned with refugees, UNHCR's work crosses over into migration issues because refugees often use the same routes and means of transports as migrants.

The International Centre for Migration Policy Development (*www.icmpd.org*): An 11-member intergovernmental organisation that seeks to "promote innovative, comprehensive and sustainable migration policies and to function as a service exchange mechanism for governments and organisations in the wider European region".

Intergovernmental Consultations on Migration, Asylum and Refugees (*www.igc.ch*; restricted access): "An informal, non-decision making forum for intergovernmental information exchange and policy debate on issues of relevance to the management of international migrator flows."

4

Education can help young migrants integrate into society, learn the local language and develop the skills they will need for the adult world. Unfortunately, their track record in schooling is mixed – some do exceptionally well, but others encounter problems that can hold them back throughout life.

Migrants and Education

By way of introduction...

One word will long be associated with the Bracken Educate Together school in Ireland – "emergency". In a country, where preparations for new schools usually begin at least 12 months – and often many years – in advance, this school was conceived, staffed and opened over just a few weeks in September 2007.

The school, housed to begin with in a summer holiday centre, is different in other ways, too. The pupils are almost all the children of migrants. They speak Pashto, Czech, Yoruba, Arabic, and many other languages. And, in a country where the bulk of the population is at least nominally Roman Catholic, the children mark the feasts of the world's major religions – Diwali, Ramadan and, of course, Christmas.

The Bracken school is a monument to many things. At one level, it represents the difficulty of finding places for non-Catholic students in a primary school system still dominated by the Catholic Church. But perhaps more significantly, the Bracken school reflects a sea change that has swept over Irish society. Over a very short period this country of emigrants has become one of immigrants: in the mid-1990s, people born overseas represented less than 3% of Ireland's population; today the figure is closer to 14%.

As the Bracken experience shows, planning for such change is difficult, and nowhere more so than in education. In some ways the questions are basic – how does a society with rapidly changing demographics find enough classrooms and teachers who can work in a multicultural environment? More profoundly, how does it ensure that schools really give migrant children the education they need to realise their full potential. Speaking to a reporter, the school's administrator, Gerry McKevitt, put the challenges facing his school this way: "This is the front line in all this. This is where the problems are emerging. This is where integration is going to happen or not."

▶ This chapter looks at the intersection of education and migration. It examines how well immigrants do in education, drawing in part on data from the OECD's PISA testing of 15-year-old students around the world. It then looks at ways in which immigrants can be helped to make up educational shortfalls. Finally, it examines the growing importance of the international student – an example of migration *for* education – and why universities and governments might like to see even more of them.

How well do migrants do in education?

Gerry McKevitt has a good point when he says that school is "where integration is going to happen or not". His school is not alone. Many OECD countries now have sizeable numbers of students from immigrant backgrounds. In Germany, France and Sweden, for example, at least one in ten 15-year-old students is a first or second-generation immigrant. In the United States it's one in six, while in Australia, New Zealand and Canada it's more than one in five.

These raw numbers conceal as much as they reveal. Just like native populations, migrants are a diverse lot, and the families of immigrant children vary greatly in terms of income, education levels, attitudes towards schooling, language abilities and much more. Still, in at least three significant ways, school can play a role in supporting migrant children:

Firstly, education helps to mould the next generation, whether native-born or migrant. Around the world and throughout history, this process is seen as key to building long-term social stability – developing shared senses of identity and communicating core values and traditions to children. This is a complex task, and even in societies that are relatively homogenous there is often fierce debate over the sort of values schools should help to transmit. In multicultural societies, this task is even more fraught, and it can raise questions over societies' core values and the extent to which immigrants should be expected to adopt them. Are they derived from religious or secular values? Do they stress the need for people to work together or to make their own way in the world? Do they seek to pass on tradition or urge an embrace of modernity?

> **"As socialising agents, schools help transmit the norms and values that provide a basis for social cohesion.
> In diverse, multi-ethnic societies, this task is not only important, but also complex."**
> *Where Immigrant Students Succeed*

These questions may sound abstract, but how they are asked and how they are answered can have implications in the real world. For example, two very different OECD countries, France and Turkey, have both struggled with debates over whether

Islamic girls and women should be allowed to wear headscarves in educational institutions. Opponents say the wearing of headscarves in state-run schools and colleges flies in the face of official secularist values. Proponents argue that not allowing girls and young women to wear headscarves leads religious families to keep them at home, thus depriving them of a full education.

Secondly, education plays a key role in the lives of migrant children when it comes to language learning, a process that can also help to form useful social bridges. And, finally, just as with native-born children, education helps immigrant children to develop the skills and competencies they will need to find jobs later on in life and to navigate their way through the adult world.

How well do schools do in educating immigrant children? Do immigrants do better – or worse – than native-born children? Over the past few years, the OECD's PISA programme for testing students around the world has been helping to answer these questions.

What is a first-generation migrant?

Immigrants who were born in another country are called first-generation immigrants. Those whose parents were born in another country, but who themselves were born in the country where their parents have settled, are known as second-generation immigrants. These distinctions are important when it comes to looking at how immigrant children are doing in education. For instance, second-generation students often speak the local language better than first-generation immigrants, and their test scores tend to be stronger, although not always markedly so. Nevertheless, PISA also shows that both first and second generation issues face many similar challenges in education.

What does PISA tell us?

PISA – the Programme for International Student Assessment – is an OECD project that tests the abilities of a sample of 15-year-old students around the world every three years. Unlike regular school exams, which usually test students to see how much of the curriculum they've absorbed, PISA is more broad ranging. It seeks to determine how well young people at the age of 15 – a point that in a number of countries marks the end of compulsory schooling – can apply their skills in reading, mathematics and science to solving real-world problems.

As well as the tests themselves, PISA also collects a very wide range of data on students' personal and family background, as well as on their motivation to learn and attitudes to school. OECD has analysed the results to see how well immigrant students are performing, and has produced a huge amount of data and information.

Here are some of the findings:

Some migrant students do well, some don't: A self-evident point, but one that bears repeating. In parts of the world, racism and xenophobic attitudes are a constant – albeit at times inaudible – backbeat in the migration debate, and they can obscure the reality that migrant students, like any other student, are individuals. Just as in the wider population, family and social background can go a long way to determining how well an individual migrant student does in school, but they're not the only factors. The student's own attitudes and personality matter a lot, and this is true of migrants just as much as native students. That said, looking at *average* performance in the PISA results shows that children from immigrant backgrounds do better in some countries than in others. Understanding why is important, as it can offer clues to how education systems can better support migrant students. But it's also important to bear in mind that because of varying country admission policies, schools in one country may not be dealing with the same sort of immigrants as those in another country: In some countries migrant families may typically be wealthier, better educated or more fluent in the local language than in others.

Migrant students want to learn: Amid the great diversity of findings from PISA, one result shows up with what OECD researchers call "striking" consistency – migrant students are at least as keen to learn, if not more so, than native-born students. There has been a lot of speculation over why this should be so. In part, it may be because people who migrate are more motivated to succeed and optimistic about the future. Whatever the reasons, the finding is important because it shows that schools have much to build on in terms of students' positive attitudes.

> **"Previous research suggests that immigrants tend to be optimistic and may therefore possess more positive learning characteristics."**
> *Where Immigrant Students Succeed*

Migrant students' performance varies between countries: In three of the traditional settlement countries – Australia, Canada and New Zealand – immigrant students did every bit as well as native students in the PISA 2006 tests. For example, in those countries about 18% of second-generation immigrants reached the highest levels (Levels 5 and 6), which was about the same as native students. But in a number of other countries, most notably Austria, Belgium, Denmark, France, Germany, the Netherlands and Sweden, they did noticeably less well. In Denmark, only about 1% of second-generation immigrants were top performers, against 7% for natives.

It's tempting to imagine that these differences might be mainly due to the likelihood that migrant students' parents in Australia are wealthier and better educated than those in Denmark. But this isn't the full answer. PISA shows striking variations in the performance of immigrant children with very similar backgrounds in different countries. For instance, in PISA 2003, immigrant students from Turkey living in Switzerland scored 31 points higher in maths than those living in Germany. This effectively means the children in Switzerland were not too far off from being a full year ahead of those in Germany, even though they were still behind native students (38 points on PISA's 600-point scale is roughly equivalent to a school year's difference). This finding is important, because it shows that schools in some countries are doing a better job of educating migrant students.

Many migrant students are struggling in school: PISA grades students in each subject area on a scale from 1 to 6, where Level 1 equals the weakest performance and Level 6 the strongest. These levels reflect more than just how well students are doing in school – they're designed to give a sense of whether students have sufficient skills to be able to make real use of them in later life. For example, can they do the sort of maths needed to work out price differences in the supermarket or to figure out interest rates on a loan? In the 2003 tests on maths skills, it was reckoned that students falling below Level 2 risked facing lifelong problems in this sort of area.

"... the long-term social and financial costs of educational inequalities can be high, as those without the competencies to participate socially and economically may not realise their potential and are likely to generate higher costs for health, income support, child welfare and security."
PISA 2006: Science Competencies for Tomorrow's World

Only very small percentages of native students failed to reach Level 2, but that wasn't true for immigrant students. In most of the countries with large immigrant populations that took part in the 2003 PISA round, around a quarter of first generation immigrant students failed to reach Level 2. In some countries, the proportion was even higher – around two out of five in Belgium, France, Norway and Sweden. These are worrying findings, as they indicate that many migrant students will face serious problems later on, including poor job prospects, low earnings and difficulties playing a full part in society.

What explains migrants' PISA performance?

What causes these variations? Why do the children of some migrants do better than others? The range of factors is wide, and they aren't always easy to disentangle from each other, but here are some of the more significant.

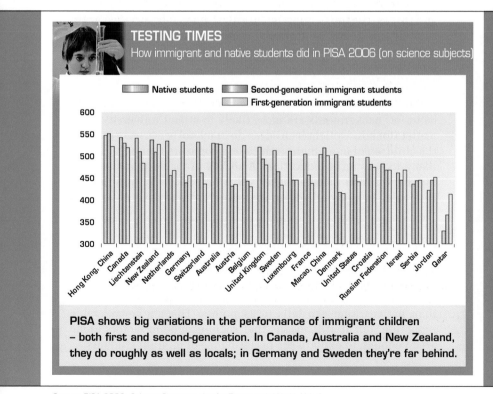

TESTING TIMES
How immigrant and native students did in PISA 2006 (on science subjects)

PISA shows big variations in the performance of immigrant children – both first and second-generation. In Canada, Australia and New Zealand, they do roughly as well as locals; in Germany and Sweden they're far behind.

Source: PISA 2006: Science Competencies for Tomorrow's World, Vol. 1.
StatLink ▄▄▄ : http://dx.doi.org/10.1787/141848881750

Country admission policies: The sort of immigrants that settle in a country makes a difference to how well migrant students do in school. For instance, some traditional permanent settlement countries like Australia use selection systems to decide who should be allowed to immigrate, grading would-be citizens for things like professional skills, language abilities and – crucially – educational qualifications. So, migrants to Australia tend to be better educated and to have higher incomes than those who go to, say, Germany. In turn, their children tend to do better in PISA testing.

Socio-economic background is important: In many ways, a student from an immigrant family is no different than one from any other family. Just as with his or her local counterparts, success in school is linked to a considerable extent to the family's social and economic status – its income levels, whether it's blue-collar or white collar, and so on. Research from PISA and around the world has consistently shown that – on average – middle-class children do better in school than children from poorer families, and this is true too of migrant children. (It must be stressed again that all this refers to *averages*; there are children from poorer families who excel in school and children from middle-class families who don't.)

Other factors are tied in with socio-economic status, especially parents' level of education. For example, people who come from better-off backgrounds are more likely to attend university. This matters for how well their children do in school because, in general, the children of more highly educated people are themselves more likely to stay on in education. Also, it's probable that the more highly educated place a higher value on education, and may be better able to help and encourage their children in their learning.

So, where immigrant students face problems in education, how much of it can be attributed to their families' socio-economic back-ground? Across the OECD area, migrant students are an average of 54 points behind native students on PISA's 600-point scale. However, when account is taken of the reality that, in many OECD countries, migrant families have lower incomes than natives, that gap falls to 34 points. That's a considerable reduction, but it still means that socio-economic factors alone aren't enough to explain the performance of migrant students.

> "... relative performance levels of students with
> an immigrant background cannot solely be attributed
> to the composition of immigrant populations in terms
> of their educational and socio-economic background."
>
> *PISA 2006: Science Competencies for Tomorrow's World*

Language: Mastering the language of instruction plays an important role in how well students do, especially those who were born in another country (first-generation immigrants). Generally, students who speak a foreign language at home do less well in PISA tests. In a number of European countries, such as Germany, Switzerland and the Netherlands, such students performed between 82 and 102 points lower in science in the PISA 2006 round. However in some of the permanent settlement countries, Australia and Canada, the gap is smaller – only around 19 to 23 points. Once again, this probably reflects that fact that immigrant families in these countries are usually wealthier and better educated than migrants in Europe. In addition, it may show that – in some cases at least – these countries are doing a better job at helping immigrant students make up language shortfalls.

Speaking a different language at home can be a benefit – there is evidence to show that early bilingualism improves people's overall language-learning abilities. But it can also hold back students. Firstly, where immigrant students are not as fluent in the local language as native students, they can find it hard to follow lessons in class and complete assignments, and they may struggle to settle into the school community. Secondly, families may not be able to help their children with their lessons. In the United States, for instance, researchers came across the case of a boy from a Mexican immigrant family who convinced his father that the failing grade "F" on his report card actually stood for "fabulous".

> "... using another language at home may indicate
> a situation of inadequate integration where parents
> do not have the skills necessary to assist with homework... "
>
> *Where Immigrant Students Succeed*

Education systems: The conditions in schools can affect student performance. So, do migrant students go to the same sorts of schools as natives? In terms of resources – school labs, computers, teacher numbers and so on – the differences don't tend to be all that great. In a few countries, such as Greece and

Denmark, school principals in schools with high numbers of migrant students say resources can be a problem; in others, such as Spain, Sweden and the United Kingdom, there may actually be more resources in such schools.

"Students from many minority groups are more likely to end up in low status tracks and streams, be more at risk of dropout, and be underrepresented among students in tertiary education. Often social background explains much of this."

No More Failures: Ten Steps to Equity in Education

However, there is one important characteristic worth noting: Immigrants are more likely to go to schools with large numbers of students from poorer families. This links back to immigrant families' socio-economic status. In most OECD countries, migrants tend to be poorer than the general population; equally, in most OECD countries, social status tends to be a factor in determining what sort of school students go to – most countries have schools that are effectively blue collar or white collar. And, in general, students in schools with lots of better-off students tend to do better. Children from poorer families are also more likely to be "streamed" into a non-academic courses than those from wealthier families, regardless of their aptitude. This streaming – both social and academic – can be very hard for students to escape from.

How can education help migrants?

Because students' success at school is so intricately tied up with their families' socio-economic background, it can be hard to come up with recommendations for changes in education that specifically target migrant needs. In most OECD countries, especially in Europe, any policies that succeed in making family background less of a factor in education are likely also to benefit migrant students.

Indeed, there may be sound political reasons for thinking about the education problems of migrant students primarily in terms of their socio-economic background. In much of the world, there's considerable public opposition to giving special treatment to immigrant families, who may be accused of "scrounging off the system". However, by not acting to help migrant students with

OECD and... Migrant education

With migrant populations growing in many developed countries, OECD is placing a new emphasis on research into migration and education, especially in trying to develop a deeper understanding of the policies that work in the education of young migrants. Already, the PISA programme is providing unique insights into how well 15-year-olds from all sorts of backgrounds – not just immigrants – are doing in education. More than 60 countries are taking part in the most recent round of PISA, in 2009, providing a wealth of data on the performance of students in education systems around the world. Now OECD is working to build on that research by examining real-world policies and practices in a number of member countries on migrant educa-tion. The Thematic Review on Migrant Education, which got under way in 2008-09, will examine the situation in five to six member countries, reviewing existing education policies to develop an understanding of what works – and what doesn't – at the national, local and school levels. Through interviews with teachers, students, parents and other key actors in education, the review aims to explore questions raised by PISA, and investigate issues outside the scope of PISA.

Why should countries be concerned about how well migrant students are doing? Aart de Geus, an OECD Deputy Secretary-General sought to answer that question in a speech at the launch of the review: "If we don't help immigrant children to succeed in school, then we impose on them a penalty that will stay with them for the rest of their lives," he said. "They will find it harder to participate in the economy, face a higher exposure to unemployment, earn less over their working lives and have lower pensions." But, he pointed out, it's sometimes difficult for governments to figure out the most appropriate policies. "The education of migrants is challenging and complex, not least because each migrant group has its own distinctive history. And so does each country..." he said. "Perhaps all this diversity explains why policy makers in many countries are grappling with the challenges and finding it difficult to figure out what can, and should, be done."

To find out more about the Thematic Review on Migrant Education, visit *www.oecd.org/edu/migration*.

To find out more about PISA, visit *www.pisa.oecd.org*.

difficulties – whether through targeted policies or a broader socio-economic approach – societies risk depriving them of the skills and education they will need to make their own way in the world and to make a full contribution in the societies they have come to call home. Ultimately, societies that fail to help migrant children to fulfil their potential through education will pay a social cost as well as a real financial price through things like higher rates of unemployment.

What can societies do to help migrant students who face problems in education? Before trying to answer that question, it needs to be stated that an education system always exists within a broader context – in any country, a school system both shapes and is shaped by deep-seated cultural and social values, history and the mix of rich and poor in society. Approaches to education in one country may not be acceptable in another. Nevertheless, looking at and comparing how countries run their education systems can be useful and eye-opening. In particular, the experiences of countries in three areas are worth briefly highlighting:

Pre-school care and education: Providing high-quality pre-school care and education can bring benefits to children no matter what their background. But it may have a special role to play for immigrant children and their families – for example, getting families involved in their children's pre-school care and education can help break down social barriers and help integrate them into the community.

> "... family involvement should also be encouraged and valued, especially the involvement of low-income and immigrant parents, who face the added challenge of segregation and exclusion."
>
> *Starting Strong II: Early Childhood Education and Care*

So, what can pre-school do for immigrant kids? Firstly, in educational terms, very young children have a powerful ability to learn languages, and not just the one spoken at home. Pre-school can help children make use of this ability, and provide a means for them to gain a firm foothold in the language of their adopted country. The early education and learning benefits go beyond just language learning: Research from the United Kingdom showed most children classified as "at risk" in terms of their social and intellectual development (which included a disproportionate number of migrant children), moved out of that category after just a year in a good nursery school.

Secondly, in development terms, pre-school can help ease the impact of family poverty. Kindergartens that combine education with care – monitoring children's health and development, ensuring they get exercise and providing sound nutrition, for instance – can bring major benefits to very young children at a crucial stage of their development. Also, providing day-care facilities can make it easier for parents to go out to work, especially mothers, which can increase family incomes and further reduce the impact of poverty.

Hard data is difficult to come by, but in many countries migrant children appear less likely to attend pre-school than their native counterparts. In some cases, that's because pre-school provision is inadequate for the entire population, not just immigrants. Alternatively, when pre-school is largely state-funded – either through grants to the kindergarten or support for parents – migrant families in some countries may have to wait some time before qualifying for such support. Also, families of irregular migrants may be unwilling to bring attention to themselves by enrolling children in pre-school. And there may be cultural objections to children attending pre-school – among some communities, it's felt that the young should be raised at home by their mothers, and not by strangers.

School support: Many countries offer special preparatory classes to young migrants, which aim to get them up to speed in their language abilities and, where necessary, in other subjects. But students' experiences in these classes differ greatly. In Spain, for instance, most students spend only a few months in such "welcome classes" before entering mainstream schooling. In others, such as Switzerland, students may spend as long as two years in special classes and still not be deemed ready to join regular schooling.

There may well be a law of diminishing returns to placing migrants in preparatory classes. Many educationalists believe it's better to keep as many students as possible in mainstream classrooms, and then target assistance to those who need it. This may help to speed up migrant students' social integration and avoid the creation of "ghettos" in education.

> **"Immigrant children with weak achievement sometimes learn faster in normal classes than in special education."**
> *No More Failures: Ten Steps to Equity in Education*

Segregation of migrant students can also show up in other areas of education. In a number of countries, migrant and minority children are more likely to be schooled in special-needs institutions: In the United States, African-American children – most of whom are *not* immigrants – are 2.5 times more likely to be diagnosed as mentally retarded than whites; in some areas of Switzerland, Hispanic children are overrepresented in special education; and in Hungary, about 40% of Roma – or Gypsy – children are classified as "mildly mentally retarded", compared with 9% of Hungarian children.

Of course, just as in the general population, some migrant and minority children do indeed suffer from real learning disabilities. However, for a number of reasons, these problems may be over-diagnosed among migrants and minorities: They may have spent less time in school than their native peers; they may have "learned" rules of behaviour from their families or native communities – boisterousness or passivity, for example – that are misinterpreted by mainstream society; or they may be victims of ethnic stereotyping. School bullying may also be an issue, which can lead to higher drop-out rates among immigrant children.

Cultural differences can be a barrier in education. But they can also be a bridge. In Sweden, one local school has sought to improve teaching for Roma children through hiring Roma teachers and staff, and by integrating elements of Roma culture into mainstream subjects. In teaching maths, examples drawn from horse-raising are widely used. Girls, meanwhile, can also learn traditional embroidery skills. Through their work with parents, Roma teachers in this *Nytorpsskolan* programme have managed to sharply reduce dropout rates.

Indeed, regardless of immigrant and minority students' background, the quality of teaching is a prime factor in their education. In some European countries that have seen sudden influxes of immigrants in recent years, such as Spain and Ireland, teachers have sometimes struggled to cope with the challenge of teaching increasing numbers of children from diverse cultural and ethnic backgrounds. With international migration likely to grow in the years to come, these are issues that more and more teachers are likely to face. Increasingly, this will need to be reflected in their training, both at the initial stages and throughout their careers.

There may also be a need to look at how schools can support immigrant families in playing a bigger role in their children's education. As we've seen, levels of parental education are a big influence on how well students do in school, but among some immigrant communities parents may have very low levels of education, especially if they come from cultures that place little emphasis on schooling for women. Schools may be able to work with such families to provide guidance on how students can be helped with homework and given space and time for study, for example. More broadly, where state resources for immigrant education are limited, schools may be able to work more closely with immigrant communities and private groups that support immigrant education to explore creative ways to support student's learning.

Language: There are a wide variety of potential approaches for schools aiming to get young immigrants up to speed in the language of their adopted countries. At the most basic level, migrant children may simply attend school like any other student and receive no special language instruction. The idea is that they will pick up the language simply through being immersed in it. These days, however, this sort of approach is rather rare.

More common is to combine immersion with special language support: Students attend regular classes as well as additional language classes. Although approaches can vary between different regions within countries and even between schools, this sort of teaching is widespread across the OECD area.

Other approaches exist, too. Students may go through a relatively short and separate intensive programme of language learning before transferring to mainstream education. In some countries, this transitional phase is broadened out to cover a wider range of academic subjects, so that students are taught bilingually for a time, and only gradually make the transition to learning full-time in their adopted language. Finally, in a very few countries, students may be helped to go on learning in both languages, with the aim of helping them to become fully bilingual. In Sweden, for instance, municipalities are legally required to provide such teaching if there are five or more children in the area with the same native language.

Language – how it's taught and whether children are encouraged to hold on to their native tongue or to adopt a new one – is a sensitive issue. It goes to the heart of identity and to the debate over how immigrants should "integrate" into their adopted country – should they be encouraged to retain their own culture or should they try to blend in to their adopted countries. Nevertheless, even if bilingualism is officially encouraged, there's widespread consensus in OECD countries on the benefits for immigrants – and especially children – in also learning the local language.

While research is still limited on what works best in helping young immigrants to do that, one thing seems clear: Countries that approach the challenge systematically – setting down clear goals and standards for language learning by young immigrants – seem to do a better job.

Migration *for* education

In recent years, a growing number of young people have been migrating – temporarily at least – to advance their education. These international students are not always considered migrants in a formal sense, but they are still having a significant economic and social impact, both on the countries they leave behind and on those in which they study. In many cases, this migration for education is also a prelude to longer stays overseas and even permanent emigration.

In 1975, it's estimated that there were around 610 000 students enrolled outside their home country. By 2005 – 30 years later – that had more than quadrupled to just over 2.7 million students. That growth is still going strong: In the early years of this decade, it's estimated that the number of international students worldwide was rising at more than 8% a year.

Where do these students come from? In the OECD area, around one in two – 47.4% – come from Asia. Within Asia, China (including Hong Kong, China) is the biggest source, accounting for around 18% of students. The next biggest source region is Europe, which accounts for about one in four international students in the OECD area, followed by Africa, about one in 10, and then South America, about one in 20. North Americans account for fewer than one in 25.

As for where they go to study, around 85% of the world's international students come to the OECD area. Within this zone, just four countries – the United States, United Kingdom, Germany and France – absorb more than half of the incoming students. Of these, the United States is by far the largest destination country – taking in more than one in five in 2005.

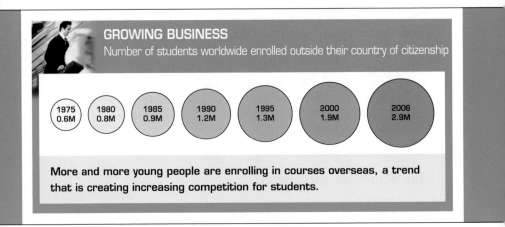

GROWING BUSINESS
Number of students worldwide enrolled outside their country of citizenship

| 1975 0.6M | 1980 0.8M | 1985 0.9M | 1990 1.2M | 1995 1.3M | 2000 1.9M | 2006 2.9M |

More and more young people are enrolling in courses overseas, a trend that is creating increasing competition for students.

Source: *Education at a Glance 2008.*

Education goes global

The increase in international students mirrors, of course, the broader phenomenon of globalisation in recent decades – a process marked by increasing flows of people, goods, services and information around the globe. Like so much else, education has become caught up in this. Not only are more young people travelling to study, but colleges and universities are also actively reaching out to new "markets" overseas.

Talking about "markets" in education may seem crass. After all, education continues to be regarded in most of the world as a social necessity that is funded – at least in part – from the public purse and which brings benefits that cannot be measured simply in economic terms. And yet, there's little doubt that economics is an increasingly important driver in the internationalisation of education.

Back in the 1970s, overseas study was mainly seen as a way to foster social, cultural and academic links between countries and individuals, especially in the states that would go on to form the European Union and within the two major political groupings of the time, the US-led West and its allies and the Soviet-led Eastern bloc. Even today, more than 100 000 students in Europe take part every year in the Erasmus exchange programme (although these exchanges usually run for no longer than an academic term).

However, since the end of the Cold War, and on the back of the broader trend towards globalisation, colleges and universities have become increasingly keen to move out into other countries – spurred in part by commercial factors. Institutions in many developed countries now offer "remote education" courses to students who choose to study in their home countries, and are even setting up campuses overseas. Monash University, Australia's biggest, has campuses in both South Africa and Malaysia, where students can complete degrees without ever stepping foot in Australia.

Governments, too, are paying increasing attention to international education, for various reasons. Firstly, offering places to foreign students can help foster promote international mutual understanding, both between countries and within today's increasingly multicultural societies. The presence of international students on campus can widen both their own horizons and those of local students, and provide fresh perspectives and impetus for research. It can also help to establish personal links between young people who may one day go on to form part of their own countries' political and economic elites.

> "Governments ... are more actively promoting the
> international mobility of students and teachers for a mix
> of cultural, political, labour market and trade reasons."
> *Internationalisation and Trade in Higher Education*

Secondly, international students are big business. In the United States alone, one independent institute estimated that foreign students made a net contribution to the US economy in the 2006/07 academic year of $14.5 billion. As seen earlier, the United States is the biggest destination for students travelling overseas, but its share of the market is falling. Looking at enrolments of international students worldwide (and not just in the OECD area), in 2000 the United States took in around 26%; five years later, that had slipped to around 22%. In part, this fall reflects tightened rules for entry following the September 11 attacks in 2001. But it also reflects increasing competition from other English-speaking countries, most notably New Zealand, which saw its share of the international market rise six-fold to 3% over the same period.

New Zealand, as well as neighbouring Australia, are attracting more international students in part because they boast two of the major factors that influence where students choose to study: They speak English and – in relative terms, at least – they're near to where the bulk of students come from, Asia. Worldwide, students mainly go to countries where they will be taught in a language that's widely spoken. And although there are exceptions, such as the huge numbers of Chinese who go to study in North America, students generally don't like to stray too far from home. In Europe, most prefer not to leave the continent – in large part, perhaps, because EU rules mean their fees are lower there.

There's a third reason why countries are increasingly seeking to lure international students – skilled migration. For many young people, studying overseas is just the first step to a longer sojourn in another country, and some governments actively encourage them to stay: Every year, the United States sets aside 20 000 H-1Bs – a type of visa for highly skilled migrants – for foreign graduates of United States colleges.

However, in both the United States and Canada it's academic institutions – not governments – that play the biggest role in attracting overseas students. In Europe, by contrast, governments are often more directly involved in higher education, and they also often play a big part in trying to lure foreign talent.

PERSONAL VIEW Jeevan

Born in Nepal, Jeevan has studied law in both India and United States, and now lives and works in New York. (He has asked not to be identified by his full name.)

About a decade after graduation, only 10 or so of Jeevan's 80 classmates from his elite Kathmandu boarding school are still in Nepal. Ten have gone to India, another 10 to Europe and Australia – and about 30 have, like Jeevan himself, left for the United States.

Jeevan first left Nepal at age 17 to continue his education in India, at a school chosen by his father, a prominent lawyer. All five astrologers in his home town had predicted that once he turned 18, Jeevan would become driven to succeed, and they were right. But after five years of law school in Bangalore and two years at a firm in New Delhi, "I was getting really bored without challenges," Jeevan recalls. So he applied and was accepted to a one-year post-graduate programme in the United States.

The cultural contrast was much sharper this time. Some customs – like having women greet him with a kiss on the cheek – felt awkward at first. Comparing the cost of a meal with one back home was "a financial shock". The students seemed to separate into certain groups – North Americans with Britons, and Europeans with South Americans and Australians. Culinary motives brought the Asian students together.

Jeevan spent a while observing the people around him – how they talked, how they dressed, what and how they ate and drank – trying to participate, to blend in. Jeevan now works at a law firm in New York. He enjoys the challenges of his job, the variety of his new lifestyle, the efficiency and professionalism that he sees as central to the American system. But while he finds much to admire in American society, it can also be cold and impersonal – it is hard to make friends, particularly with white Americans. Unlike in Nepal or India, where doing things to help out friends and acquaintances is the norm, here "I find myself thinking very hard before asking a favour," Jeevan explains.

And personal schedules are more rigid – you can't just call up a colleague to go for dinner in an hour, it needs to be planned days in advance. When it comes to friendship, "it's easier to deal with other immigrants".

Will he go home to Nepal? Years of political crisis there have fuelled the mass emigration that Jeevan is a part of. But it's also a reason for him to go back and turn things around. The same astrologer who predicted Jeevan's successful academic turn and the year in which he would move to the United States also forecast that he would "move continents" again, so perhaps a change is at hand.

Germany and France are just two of a number of European countries that have set up special programmes to strengthen the international appeal of their higher education and research systems, particularly in science and technology. Approaches can include offering direct support to would-be students, including scholarships, and running educational consulting services.

> "Cross-border education is used in a strategic way in order to attract skilled students that may become skilled immigrants…"
>
> *Internationalisation and Trade in Higher Education:*
> *Opportunities and Challenges*

A "brain drain"?

There is, of course, a potential downside to international education. Countries that send students abroad can find themselves at risk of a longer term "brain drain" of academic talent, depriving them of researchers and – ultimately – workers in key sectors of their economy, such as information technology and medicine. Although this is sometimes portrayed as an issue mainly for developing countries, it's one that is causing concern in developed countries, especially in Europe. A study by the European Commission in 2003 showed three-quarters of European postgraduates studying in the United States wanted to stay on there after completing their doctorates, in large part because they felt the United States offered better career and employment opportunities.

Developing countries face similar concerns about a brain drain of talent (see Chapter 6), but there can be benefits, too, from sending students overseas. Students from smaller countries – at every level of development – can gain access to courses and research facilities that are unavailable at home. Indeed, such approaches to "capacity building" – in this context, the idea of helping developing countries to build a reservoir of well-trained workers in areas like technology, engineering and medicine – can form part of international development aid. But developing countries are also taking the initiative. Malaysia has an extensive programme of scholarships to train teachers, academics and public servants overseas, mainly in the United Kingdom and Australia, and it even has offices in some countries to help its citizens studying abroad.

Ready for life

This chapter has looked at the role of education in the lives of young immigrants. Crucially, as well as giving them the knowledge and skills they will need to build their lives in a new country, education also lays the groundwork for migrants' job prospects. The next chapter will look at immigrants and work – how well they do in finding jobs, the role of work in helping immigrants to integrate, and controversies over the impact of immigration on native workers.

Find Out More

FROM OECD...

On the Internet
For an introduction to PISA, visit
www.oecd.org/PISA.

To find out more about OECD's review
of migrant education, go to
www.oecd.org/edu/migration.

Publications

**PISA 2006: Science Competencies for
Tomorrow's World (2008):** Presents the
results from the most recent PISA survey,
which focused on science and also assessed
mathematics and reading. It is divided into
two volumes: the first offers an analysis
of the results, the second contains the
underlying data.

**Where Immigrant Students Succeed:
A Comparative Review of Performance and
Engagement in PISA 2003 (2006):** Based
on results from the 2003 PISA round, this
report examines the performance of students
from immigrant backgrounds. It looks
at countries' approaches to the integration
of immigrants, and at other factors that can
influence how immigrant students
do in school, such as their motivation
and learning strategies, social background
and the language spoken at home.

**No More Failures: Ten Steps to Equity in
Education (2007):** This report challenges
the assumption that there will always
be young people who can't or won't make
it in school. It looks at how different countries
have handled equity in education, including
responding to the special needs
of migrants and minorities.

**Starting Strong II: Early Childhood
Education and Care (2006):** This report
reviews early childhood education and care in
20 OECD countries, and describes the social,
economic, conceptual and research

factors that influence early childhood policy.
It includes discussions of the potential
for preschool care in helping immigrant
children overcome difficulties
in their later education.

**Internationalisation and Trade in Higher
Education: Challenges and Opportunities
(2004):** This report brings together
statistics, case studies and policy reports
on the major trends and developments
in cross-border post-secondary education
in North America, Europe,
and the Asia Pacific region.

For an introduction to OECD work
on managing migration flows, go to
www.oecd.org/migration, and follow the
link to "international migration policies".

... AND OTHER SOURCES

A number of academic centres and think
tanks work on migration-related issues.
They include the following:

**Institute for the Study of International
Migration,** at Georgetown University,
Washington DC
(*www12.georgetown.edu/sfs/isim*).

Centre on Migration Policy and Society,
at the University of Oxford, UK
(*www.compas.ox.ac.uk*).

Migration Policy Institute, in
Washington DC (*www.migrationpolicy.org*).
A think tank whose projects include
the **Migration Information Source**
(*www.migrationinformation.org*).

Migrinter, at the University
of Poitiers, France
(*www.mshs.univ-poitiers.fr/migrinter*).

**Quebec Metropolis Centre – Immigration
and Metropolis** (*www.im.metropolis.net*),
in Quebec, Canada; research consortium
of six Quebec universities.

Migrants and Work

Visit a hospital in a typical developed country and you will quickly see the roles played by migrants – everything from performing surgery to washing floors. Migrants can be a key addition to the workforce, even if their presence may sometimes be resented and they are not always able to make the best use of their skills.

By way of introduction...

Ahmet Elomari is a 37-year-old Moroccan immigrant in Canada. He has studied aerospace engineering in both Morocco and France, and has also worked in both countries. His current job? Assembling plastic toys.

When Elomari first moved to Canada, he sent out his CV to a number of companies. "I applied for many jobs at Bombardier and Air Canada, and I never even got a reply," he told *The Gazette* newspaper in Montreal. "They could have at least called."

Elomari's French qualifications were accepted by potential employees in Canada, but he says he was told constantly that he lacked relevant local work experience. "I had so many interviews and there's always an excuse – you don't speak English, you have a foreign diploma, you have no Canadian experience," he says. "How can you get Canadian experience if you don't work?" Elomari is now studying for a degree in Canada. "At least I'll eliminate some of the pretexts recruiters used on me."

Such experiences are not unusual, and nor are they restricted to immigrants in Canada. Throughout the world, immigrants face major difficulties in establishing their work credentials in their new homes. Employers, meanwhile, struggle to determine whether the skills and qualifications of migrants really are equivalent to those of local job-seekers – degrees, diplomas and certificates don't always travel well, and the further they go the less well they travel. Migrants may also face questions when it comes to previous work experience – employers are far more impressed by experience gained with local companies than with firms overseas. Add in problems with the local language, cultural barriers, lack of social contacts and discrimination, and it's not surprising than many immigrants struggle to find jobs, and often do work for which – on paper at least – they are overqualified.

▶ This chapter looks at the track record of immigrants in the jobs market – the numbers who find work and the numbers who are doing jobs that don't match their qualifications. It then looks at the impact of immigrants on local workers, and whether they bring benefits to the economy, before examining the obstacles immigrants face in finding work, and policies that can help to lower some of these barriers.

How well do migrants do in finding work?

We've seen that countries take very different approaches to the question of the social and cultural integration of immigrants, but when it comes to the narrower issue of getting immigrants into the workforce – labour market integration – governments tend to be more in agreement. By and large, they want to get immigrants working. Sometimes this is driven by economic needs: Some sectors of the economy, such as hotels, restaurants and agricultural, rely heavily on immigrant labour. But there are also benefits for immigrants: Encouraging them into work can help ensure that they and their families don't get sucked into poverty traps and helps them build social and community links.

However, many immigrants encounter problems in finding work, and these are not restricted solely to first-generation migrants. Problems in the job market – as well as in education and in social integration – extend well beyond the first wave of immigrants to include their children and even their grandchildren. The risks of such exclusion were starkly set out in the OECD report, *From Immigration to Integration*, and are worth quoting:

> As the population facing problems integrating into the labour market widens, the problem of integration itself becomes more complex. Immigrants suffering from poverty as a result of labour market exclusion can become concentrated in areas of low housing cost, which are often isolated from employment opportunities. In more extreme cases, immigrants become 'ghettoised' in areas of high deprivation, with associated high rates of [joblessness], high school drop-out rates and problems of disaffection. Issues associated with social and economic exclusion in this case form a set of additional barriers for immigrants seeking to access the labour market.

How many immigrants find work?

It's not surprising that the success – and otherwise – of immigrants in finding work varies greatly between countries, even for immigrants who come from the same country or region. Success in the jobs market also varies for different types of immigrants. For example, refugees and asylum seekers seem to face particular problems. Unlike other migrants, who may reflect

What are "employment" and "unemployment"?

Economists use a number of different terms to discuss how many people in a country are working, not working or looking for work. The most familiar of these is probably the unemployment rate, which indicates the percentage of people of working age – roughly between the ages of 18 and 65 – who are unemployed and looking for work. Two other terms are also frequently used:
> The employment rate is the percentage of people of working age who are actually working.
> The participation rate is similar but adds a second crucial element:

it's the percentage of people of working age who are working or looking for work. Why make this distinction? Mainly, because not everyone who is out of work is looking for work. In some countries and among certain immigrant groups, quite large numbers of people opt to stay out of the workforce. Among certain migrant and ethnic communities, for instance, there may be cultural barriers to women working. So, comparing participation rates between countries or between different social groups – such as migrants and locals or men and women – gives an insight into what share of a country's potential workers are actually in the workforce.

long and hard on which location offers the best job prospects before making a final decision, survival is often the main priority for refugees and there isn't always much time for planning.

In terms of having a job – or their employment rate – immigrants did about as well, and sometimes better, than locals in about half the 24 countries for which the OECD has reliable data for the years in the run up to the 2008 recession. This was the case in parts of southern Europe that saw big upsurges in immigration in recent years, such as Greece and Spain, and in some other European countries, such as Austria, France and Switzerland. In the United States, locals were more likely to be in work than immigrants, but only very marginally so, while the gaps were larger in Australia and Canada. The gaps got bigger still in Northern Europe, where a history of humanitarian migration means some immigrants have little schooling and only a weak grasp of the language. In Denmark, for instance, about four out of five people in the general population had jobs, but this fell to only around two out of three immigrants.

But such broad numbers can obscure some big variations *within* the immigrant population. For example, the proportion of immigrant women who work is always lower than that for immigrant men, and it's also generally lower compared with local women. It's true that, in general, women are less likely to do paid work than men, but among certain immigrant groups this situation may be exacerbated by special factors, including cultural resistance to the idea of women working. Some immigrant women may face additional pressure to remain at home if their families must first go through a waiting period before qualifying for state-subsidised childcare.

> **"Immigrant women are generally the group with the least favourable outcomes in the labour markets..."**
> *International Migration Outlook: SOPEMI 2007*

As we saw earlier, the children of immigrants – the second-generation – can also encounter problems integrating into society and into the job market. Although they do better than young first-generation immigrants – new arrivals – they don't do as well as young locals. In the Nordic countries and other parts of northern Europe, they seem to face especially large problems.

The children of immigrants can also suffer because of their parents' educational background. We've seen that parents' income and education levels usually affect how well their children do in school and, thus, their future employment prospects. Among some immigrant groups in Europe, education levels are markedly

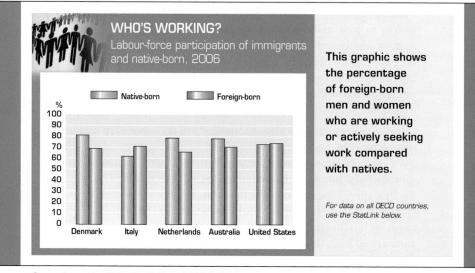

WHO'S WORKING?
Labour-force participation of immigrants and native-born, 2006

This graphic shows the percentage of foreign-born men and women who are working or actively seeking work compared with natives.

For data on all OECD countries, use the StatLink below.

Source: *International Migration Outlook: SOPEMI 2008.*

StatLink : *http://dx.doi.org/10.1787/427830451278*

lower than among the general population. It's perhaps inevitable that some of this educational disadvantage is passed on to the second-generation and that, combined with other factors such as discrimination, it creates real problems for these young people as they try to enter the workforce.

What about unemployment, or the number of immigrants actively seeking work but unable to find it? Although the situation has generally improved in recent years, immigrants are more likely to be unemployed than locals across the OECD area, with the exception of the United States and one or two other countries. In the Nordic area, the unemployment rate of immigrants is about twice that of locally born people. Long-term unemployment – where people have been seeking work for more than a year – is also a problem, with migrants tending to be at greater risk. That's worrying, as the longer people are out of work, the harder it is for them to get back into work, so long-term unemployment can represent an additional employment barrier to immigrants.

> "Immigrants usually continue to be over-represented among the unemployed, notably the long-term unemployed."
> *International Migration Outlook: SOPEMI 2007*

What sort of work do immigrants do? Visit the theatres and wards of hospitals in most wealthy countries, and you'll see immigrants doing all sorts of work – from highly-specialised surgery, to nursing, to mopping floors. From a less anecdotal perspective, it's useful to look at how many immigrants are working in various sectors compared with locals – in other words, are they under or over-represented. In general – and accepting that there are big differences between countries – immigrants tend to be more prevalent in the construction, hotel and restaurant sectors, as well as in healthcare and social services, such as caring for the elderly.

Immigrants also tend to be more likely to do temporary and part-time jobs – in Spain, more than half of immigrants, about 56%, have only temporary work, compared with 31% of locals. And, increasingly, immigrants are becoming self-employed. The reasons for this vary: It could indicate that immigrants are becoming well-established in their adopted countries and have the financial means to set up businesses; or it could be a sign that the barriers to finding a job are so high that it's easier for them to work for themselves.

How does immigration affect local workers?

One of the most widely heard accusations against immigrants is that they take jobs from locals, usually – it's claimed – because they are willing to work for less. How true are such claims, and do immigrants really harm the job prospects of natives?

As with so much else in international migration, there are no simple answers to these questions. The situation varies from country to country and from occupation to occupation – whether the immigrants and natives are low or high-skilled workers. The answers also depend on timeframes – immigrants may have a short-term, but little long-term, impact – and whether we look at the state of the job market nationally or in a particular city or region.

None of this means that immigrants don't have an impact on native workers' jobs. All it is saying is that this impact isn't always easy to measure. Regrettably, in the absence of clear-cut data, rumour and anecdote may fill the gap, leading to the classic accusation against immigrants that "they're coming over here to steal our jobs".

What's the reality? Arguably, immigrants can help some local workers: For instance, if a family hires a migrant to care for children, it may allow both parents to go out to work. Or, if a

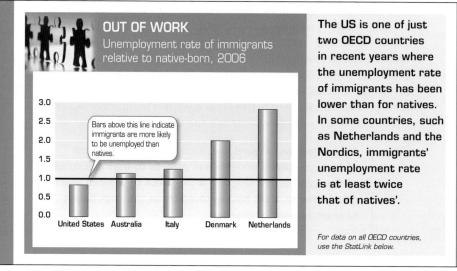

OUT OF WORK

Unemployment rate of immigrants relative to native-born, 2006

Bars above this line indicate immigrants are more likely to be unemployed than natives.

3.0
2.5
2.0
1.5
1.0
0.5
0.0

United States   Australia   Italy   Denmark   Netherlands

The US is one of just two OECD countries in recent years where the unemployment rate of immigrants has been lower than for natives. In some countries, such as Netherlands and the Nordics, immigrants' unemployment rate is at least twice that of natives'.

For data on all OECD countries, use the StatLink below.

Source: International Migration Outlook: SOPEMI 2008.

StatLink ▨▧▦ : *http://dx.doi.org/10.1787/427620785702*

restaurant hires migrants as waiting staff it may be able to expand its business, creating new jobs for managers that may well go to locals. Economists also argue that immigrants can complement native workers by doing work locals are unwilling to do, the so-called "3D jobs" – dirty, dangerous and difficult. In the United Kingdom, for instance, a BBC television programme interviewed Polish farm workers picking crops in the fields as well as some local men who were collecting social benefits. The Poles were paid £7, or a little less than $14, an hour, and seemed pleased with the work. "It's wonderful here," said one. But at the state-benefits office, locals derided the work. "No mate I'd prefer to sign-on [for benefits] than do that," said one man, adding: "I don't want to work in like no cornfield. I don't want to work with a load of foreigners."

As well as highlighting some xenophobic attitudes, the man's response hints at another accusation that's often made against immigrants, namely that their willingness to work for less drives down salaries – in some cases, to such an extent that locals just won't do the work anymore. There is some evidence that migrants do push down wages, but many economists argue that the impact is pretty small and that it doesn't last all that long. Those who are hit worst tend to be lower-skilled – and, thus, lower-paid – workers, and these usually include earlier waves of migrants.

It's also sometimes argued that an influx of immigrants is an easy solution that allows governments and employers to avoid systematically tackling deep-seated labour shortages by, for instance, raising salaries or boosting training opportunities for locals. Some argue that this situation already exists in many OECD countries when it comes to nursing and medicine. The availability of foreign nurses, especially temporary workers, means there's little pressure on salaries to rise or on hospitals to improve working conditions to encourage more locals to enter the profession.

> **"… some have argued that temporary employment of foreign nurses undermines efforts to improve conditions and wages for nurses, *i.e.* it prevents developed country governments from having to address the root cause of their nursing shortages."**
>
> *Trade and Migration*

How does immigration affect the economy?

There's another aspect of the impact of immigrants that's almost as controversial, namely do they help or hurt the economies of the countries in which they go to live? It's an interesting question, but some observers question whether it's the right one to ask. As Chapter 3 showed, a large slice of legal immigration in many countries is essentially beyond government control. If such migration is going to happen anyway, arguing over whether it helps or hinders the economy may be of limited relevance. Nevertheless, such debates are going on in many countries, and it's worth taking a moment to look at the issues.

What's clear, firstly, is that the economics of such questions are complex, and to some extent they come down to issues of definition. Defined over the course of the history of a country like the United States, immigration has clearly brought huge economic and social benefits. Defined over the shorter term – and this is the sort of time-frame that such debates usually focus on – the results may be more ambiguous.

Secondly, these debates are also often shaped by questions of measurement. For instance, immigrants are key workers in certain industries, such as hotels or restaurants. Without them, many employers argue they couldn't operate, or at least not at their current level. So, immigrant workers can enable businesses to expand. That should add up to an increase in economic activity, but how should that be measured? In terms of how fast the economy is growing overall, or in terms of whether people's incomes are rising, or in terms of whether *local* people's incomes are rising?

Such questions might sound arcane, but they can become significant political issues. For instance, in the United Kingdom, an all-party parliamentary committee decided that it wasn't particularly useful to measure the economic impact of migration in terms of GDP or GDP per capita. (The first of these, GDP, stands for gross domestic product, and it's a broad measure of the size of an economy; if GDP is rising, it means the economy is expanding. GDP per capita represents the size of an economy divided by the size of the population.)

Instead, the committee urged the British government to "focus on the per capita income of the resident population" – in effect, it wanted to know if immigration was actually helping to raise the incomes of natives rather than simply fuelling overall economic growth. The committee found that immigration had had only a very small impact on Britain's GDP per capita, and that – in terms or residents' incomes – it had slightly hurt the lowest earners and slightly benefited the highest. The findings were widely reported in the British media, with one newspaper running its coverage under the headline, "Migration has brought 'zero' economic benefit".

"… reaching a conclusion on the impact of migration on output and, especially, output per head is as much a matter for speculation as for calculation."
OECD Economic Surveys: Greece, 2005

In the United States, too, economists have debated the economic impact of immigration – and come close to blows. One economist recalls trying to calm down a "shouting match" between two other leading economists debating just such a question at a conference: "It was like, 'guys, go up to the room and punch each other out'," he told *The Wall Street Journal*.

One of those arguing economists was George J. Borjas, who emigrated from Cuba in the 1960s and went on to become a professor at Harvard. He argues that, on balance, "immigration is neither a huge boon for the United States nor a huge drain". In that he is echoed by many other economists, including some who favour a more open immigration policy than Borjas does. Where he differs from many of his colleagues is in arguing that immigrants have a serious impact on the earnings of Americans, particularly those of unskilled workers. Other economists believe this overstates the case. For instance, David Card, a professor at Berkeley (and an emigrant from Canada), argues that there is "limited evidence of adverse effects on less skilled natives".

The United States is just one economy, so what about the economic impact of migration elsewhere? Inevitably, the answer varies, but overall – and just as in the United States and the United Kingdom – it's not thought to be all that great, either in positive or negative terms. One study of a number of countries found that the short-term impact of immigration on annual GDP was only around plus or minus 0.5%. Over the longer term, the impact probably tends to be positive, albeit still not all that substantial. (Bear in mind also that there may be what economists call a "mechanical" impact from migration on GDP. In simple terms, an increase in the size of country's population – whether from rising birth rates or increasing migration – usually automatically adds up to more economic activity, which is reflected in increased GDP.)

Several factors help determine the impact of an immigrant on the economy, one of the most important being whether or not he or she has a job, especially one requiring high skills levels. Immigrants who find work contribute far more to the economy than those who don't. This is one reason why immigration tends to bring more economic benefits in the traditional settlement countries, like Australia, where the right to enter is often determined by the likelihood of an immigrant finding work.

> **"The weak labour force participation among immigrants in Northern Europe is [...] the main factor driving the estimated negative fiscal impact of immigration."**
> *Jean, S. et al. in "Migration in OECD Countries"*

By contrast, in some countries in Northern Europe, immigrants can be more of a burden on the economy, in large part because of their relatively high levels of unemployment. It's thus important – both for the national economic and for their own economic prospects – that migrants are helped to enter the labour force, and that they do jobs that match their skills and education. Unfortunately, this is an area where migrants often encounter serious obstacles.

Is migrants' human capital being wasted?

In recent decades, the concept of human capital (*see box*) has come to be used widely by economists and politicians – and in a somewhat narrower sense in the business world – to express the idea that people and governments can invest in education and training, and that this investment brings rewards, in terms of increased incomes and higher economic productivity.

Human capital is a useful concept for helping to explain how well immigrants are doing in the workforce, not just in terms of having a job, but whether or not they're doing a job that really matches their education and training. In many cases, immigrants in OECD countries are ostensibly overqualified for the work they're doing, and not getting maximum returns on their human capital – and nor are the economies of their adopted countries.

However, it is important to note some complexities and grey areas that this term "overqualification" may obscure. A qualification that is good in one country may not really be equivalent to one from another country. Someone who gets an architecture degree

What is human capital?

In simple terms, **human capital** refers to the learning, skills, knowledge and attributes – including health and personality characterisics – of individuals and national workforces. National economies and individuals can "invest" in aspects of human capital. From the national perspective that can mean spending on schools and colleges; from the individual perspective, it can mean spending money on course fees and sacrificing the chance to earn money by remaining on in college or university.

Such investments yield returns – for economies, in the form of higher productivity and growth, and for individuals, in the form of higher incomes. Just as human capital can be created, it can be wasted, too. For example, where the qualifications and experience of immigrants are not properly recognised, they may wind up working in jobs for which they are overqualified – in other words, they're not getting a full return on their human capital.

in a developing country may not do the same training as an architecture student in, say, Northern Europe. It isn't simply a question of academic standards; the European student may have learnt about designing buildings for cold weather or may have been trained in the latest computer-aided-design software. A student in a poorer country that has less money to spend on education may not have access to such software, and may have learned to design buildings for a very different climate.

Bearing all that in mind, how well educated are migrants? Confusingly, they can be both more *and* less educated than the general population. What this means is that in many OECD countries there is often a large group of immigrants with higher levels of education than the local population, but also a large group with lower levels. Take the United Kingdom, where just over 34% of immigrants have third-level qualifications – typically, university degrees – against just over 29% of locals. But, at the other end of the education range, around 22% of immigrants finished their education before or at around the age of 16, compared with just under 16% of locals.

> "... the educational attainment of immigrants is not improving as fast as that of the native-born."
> *International Migration Outlook: SOPEMI 2008*

An interesting trend in recent years is that new immigrants tend to be better educated than previous waves of immigrants, and are increasingly likely to be college graduates. However, the education levels of native-born people are rising too – and generally at a faster pace than those of migrants. The result is that on average across the OECD area the education gap between locals and migrants is actually growing (although this is not true of every country). Nevertheless, the fact remains that migrants are more likely to have reasonable levels of education than in the past, which makes it all the more important to ensure that their skills and education are put to good use.

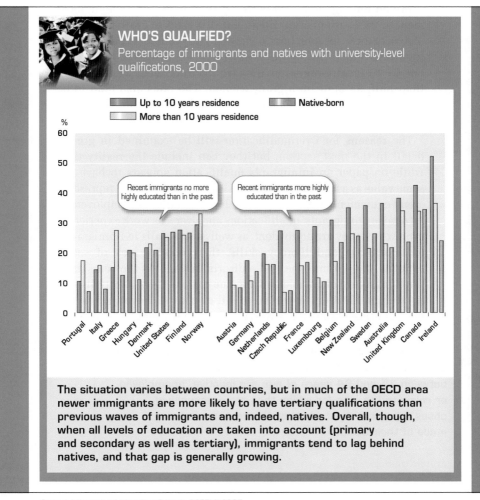

WHO'S QUALIFIED?
Percentage of immigrants and natives with university-level qualifications, 2000

Legend:
- Up to 10 years residence
- More than 10 years residence
- Native-born

Recent immigrants no more highly educated than in the past

Recent immigrants more highly educated than in the past

The situation varies between countries, but in much of the OECD area newer immigrants are more likely to have tertiary qualifications than previous waves of immigrants and, indeed, natives. Overall, though, when all levels of education are taken into account (primary and secondary as well as tertiary), immigrants tend to lag behind natives, and that gap is generally growing.

Source: *International Migration Outlook: SOPEMI 2007.*
StatLink : *http://dx.doi.org/10.1787/015032154880*

Overqualification

Unfortunately, as we've seen, this doesn't always happen. Indeed, overall, immigrants tend to do jobs that don't make the most of their skills and education. In economic terms, this overqualification means that neither they nor the societies they are now living in are getting maximum returns on their human capital.

Overqualification isn't restricted to immigrants. In most economies it also affects local workers, but it's much more common among immigrants. In Spain, about one in four local men, or 24%, are overqualified, but this rises to close to two out of five, or 39%, for men born overseas. The problem is particularly high for women immigrants: In Greece for instance, just under one in 10 local women, or 9%, are overqualified, against more than half, 53%, of immigrant women. The rates also tend to be higher for people who came originally from outside the OECD area, rather than those who migrated within the area.

The reasons for overqualification will be examined in greater detail in the next section, but they can include the reality that, while on paper an immigrants qualification appears to have the same value as a local's, in reality the learning and skills it represents aren't equivalent. They can also include the failure of employers to recognise immigrants' qualifications and overseas work experience, even where they are equivalent, as well as shortfalls in immigrants' local-language and literacy skills, their relative lack of social contacts and – it must be said – discrimination. As the years pass, immigrants are often able to overcome some of these shortfalls and so overqualification rates tend to fall over time. Nevertheless, the extent of these problems is worrying, especially for OECD societies that may already be short of skilled workers.

"... the fact that in all of the countries considered, at least 25%, and on average nearly 50%, of skilled immigrants between 15 and 64 years of age are inactive, unemployed or relegated to jobs for which they are overqualified, poses the question of whether the best use is being made of their skills."

International Migration Outlook: SOPEMI 2007

MIGRATION IN A RECESSION   The world of work

The slowdown that has swept through the world's economies has put jobs under increasing pressure, affecting both native workers and migrants. However, for a number of reasons, including because of the sort of work they do and the conditions under which they work, migrants have been hardest hit. The downturn follows a strong period for jobs in the OECD area. Between 2003 and 2007, 30 million new jobs were created, many of which were filled by migrants. Now, this impressive track record is under threat. Why?

The 'wrong' jobs

Firstly in any recession, not all jobs are equally at risk – some, such as those in construction, tend to be less secure than others, such as those in health care. In many countries, immigrants are especially likely to work in sectors that lose jobs during downturns. For example, in Greece and Spain, up to about half of working immigrants are employed in the vulnerable sectors of construction, wholesale, and hotels and catering.

But it isn't just the jobs they do that determine whether migrants stay in work. Other factors come into play, too. For example, immigrants tend to do more temporary work than natives – in some European countries, the share of immigrants in temporary employment exceeds that of natives by 50%. However, when employers need to make job cuts during recessions, temporary workers are the first to be targeted.

'Last in, first out'

Of course, businesses also let permanent staff go, too, but once again this can be bad news for migrants for a number of reasons. Firstly, companies may axe staff on the basis of "last in, first out" – that means firing their newest hires, who can often include a disproportionate number of immigrants. Discrimination may also play a part. One study in Sweden showed that during the crisis of the early 1990s, even when other factors such as seniority and job sectors were taken into account, non-European immigrants were twice as likely to be axed as natives.

Self-employment is another area of risk: In some countries, migrants are more likely to be self-employed than native workers, often running businesses that are very small, which puts them especially at risk, and in vulnerable sectors like hotels and catering.

Policy responses

As this chapter explains, most countries now work to help immigrants integrate into the workforce by offering training, retraining and language instruction. But as budgets tighten during the recession, such programmes may come under pressure. However, delaying or reducing such efforts, or reducing anti-discrimination efforts, risks long-term economic and social effects if it makes it harder for immigrants to find work.

Barriers to finding good jobs

We've seen that although newcomers to the OECD area are tending to be better educated than in the past, there are still large numbers of immigrants in many countries with relatively low levels of education. This partially explains why immigrants are generally less likely to be in work than locals, but it doesn't explain everything. For example, in France, one in two adult immigrants does not have an upper secondary education – in other words, they weren't in school long past the age of 16 – and fewer immigrants have jobs than locals. However, statistical analysis shows even if immigrants were as well educated as locals in France, about 60% of that gap in employment would remain. So, what else is preventing immigrants from entering the workforce?

Language: Immigrants don't always need a very strong grasp of the local language to find work. Indeed, in many developed countries, a whole range of low-skilled work is done by migrants with fairly basic language skills. Think of the armies of men and women who clean out shops and offices in the evenings, long after the locals have gone home, or who work as short-order cooks in cafes and restaurants, or who hold down jobs in businesses that deal mainly with their own ethnic community. Indeed, some of the biggest migration waves in recent decades involved workers with often only rudimentary skills in the local tongue, for example the Turkish guestworkers who went to Germany in the years after the Second World War.

> "Conceivably, the most important human capital component with respect to integration is the extent of knowledge of the host country language."
>
> *Jobs for Immigrants, Volume 1*

For all that, language skills do matter. Some of those unseen cleaners have the skills and education to do more high-powered work, but are prevented from doing so by their relative inability to communicate. Equally, many migrants with low skill levels never find work, and problems with the local language are often the main reason. For higher-skilled migrants, these questions are becoming even more significant. Technology is changing the jobs that many people do, and "soft skills" – such as being able to communicate fluently, make presentations and write reports – are becoming more important, placing an even greater premium on being able to speak the local lingo.

These barriers tend to be more significant in some smaller countries, such as Denmark and Sweden, simply because their languages are seldom spoken outside their shores and immigrants are unlikely to have any previous grounding in them. That's not to say that immigrants to countries where better-known languages are spoken, such as English, Spanish or French, don't also experience problems. Evidence from research in the United States, for instance, suggests that adult immigrants arriving without English almost never acquire the same fluency in it as native-born Americans.

Skills equivalence and recognition: Many employers are suspicious of qualifications earned in another country. They may doubt that the qualification actually exists or may not rate it as equivalent to one awarded locally. And the problem goes beyond employers. In many professions, such as medicine or the law, practitioners are required to undergo certifying examinations, but such certification is not always transferable overseas. Immigrants wanting to go on practising their profession may be required to effectively re-sit professional exams in their adopted country, which can be difficult if their training ended many years previously, or may even be asked to do their training all over again. There are similar issues with work skills, which many potential employers are slow to recognise if they were gained overseas.

Some countries, such as Australia, Sweden and Denmark, have set up special systems to assess and certify educational qualifications and work skills. But even where qualifications are fully certified, there seems to be a lingering reluctance by employers to recognise them. In Sweden, for instance, research shows that employees whose qualifications have been certified as fully equivalent to a local award still earn less than employees with the equivalent Swedish qualification.

Networking: In recent years, the idea of social capital has been attracting increasing interest among sociologists, economists and politicians. The idea gained even greater traction after the publication of *Bowling Alone*, by the political scientist Robert Putnam, which used the example of declining interest in once-popular tenpin bowling leagues in the United States to illustrate what Putnam claimed was Americans' broader disengagement from civic life. Such arguments haven't convinced everyone. While some critics accept social capital as a valid notion, they argue that there's very little that can be done in policy terms to increase it. And, even if there was, it would be hard to measure the results of such policies in a convincing way.

Still, even if social capital is tough to measure, its value is clear. Social capital – our networks, friendships, family relationships and so on – is important to many parts of our lives, including our personal happiness and our economic success. In simple terms, this can mean something as straightforward as receiving a tip-off from a friend about a job vacancy at work. Personal contacts play a major part in filling vacancies in much of the world – a study in Turin found that 57% of businesses hired employees through contacts with friends and family.

"... many job vacancies, if not necessarily closed to immigrants and their children, may be filled in such a way that the latter have little opportunity for their candidacies to be considered."
Jobs for Immigrants, Volume 1

Immigrants, however, often lack such contacts. To some extent, this may be because they "stick together", making little effort to build links with the local community. But they are also frequently the victims of exclusion. This can be accidental – immigrants who arrive as adults won't have had the chance to build friendships and relationships with locals in school and college. But it can also be quite active and discriminatory, with immigrants excluded because they are "different".

Exclusion from the social mainstream – for whatever reason – means immigrants can lack not only important bridges to potential employers but also certain skills for introducing themselves to them, for instance, the "right" way to write a CV or resume. Immigrants with no experience in the local labour market may also find it hard to identify suitable job opportunities, and may find it hard to hit the right note in job interviews – in some cultures, job candidates are expected to aggressively sell themselves; in others, employers expect them to be more modest and respectful.

Discrimination: There's no question that immigrants face discrimination in many areas of life, including when it comes to finding work, although the extent of this varies between different immigrant groups and between countries. For example, immigrants whose ethnicity, language and culture are closer to those of the local population often face less discrimination. Equally, research in the United States suggests that people who are seen as having left their countries for political reasons, such as some migrants from Cuba and Vietnam, are more sympathetically received than immigrants escaping poverty, such as those from Haiti and Mexico.

In the job market, it can be hard to untangle the impact of discrimination from other factors that hold back first-generation immigrants. It's a lot easier, though, in the case of second- and third-generation immigrants. In many cases, they have work experience, qualifications and language skills that are clearly equivalent to those of "native" job candidates. And yet, there is clear evidence that they suffer discrimination in the job market. How do we know? For some time now, the International Labour Organisation (ILO) has supervised an intriguing series of tests for discrimination in member countries. What happens is that CVs are sent out to companies from two fictional job candidates who have near-identical job qualifications but different names – one "local" and the other "foreign". The test's organisers then wait to see who is called for interview – the "foreigner" or the "local". Broadly speaking, the tests show that people from immigrant backgrounds typically apply for at least three times as many jobs before being called to interview. Indeed, an OECD report says the ILO tests "suggest the existence of significant discriminatory behaviour on the part of employers" in OECD countries.

> **"All other things being equal, this means that persons of immigrant background must make more applications to get equivalent results compared to applicants without a migration background."**
>
> *Jobs for Immigrants, Volume 1*

What policies can help migrants find work?

So, what are the best ways to overcome all these barriers? Approaches differ between countries, but a few common ideas stand out.

Language training: Learning to speak and read the local language is seen as a priority for immigrants in most OECD countries, not just to help them enter the labour force but also to encourage their integration into society. Indeed, in an increasing number of countries, immigrants must commit to taking a certain number of hours of language instruction – as well as social studies classes – before they can qualify for residency rights or citizenship.

In Norway, this idea is framed in the law as both a right and an obligation, and that mirrors the situation in many other places. Migrants intending to settle permanently are expected to learn the language and to take civics classes, but they also have a "right" to do so, and that right is financially supported by the state. In France, newly arrived immigrants intending to stay permanently sign a "welcome and integration contract" setting out their rights and responsibilities; the contract requires immigrants to respect the laws and values of

France and to attend civic training, and requires the state to honour the individual's rights and to provide language training.

How much training? Numbers vary. In Norway, immigrants must attend 250 hours of language training, and 50 hours of social studies, but in some situations they may be entitled to as much as 3 000 hours, or the equivalent of almost 1½ year of full-time study (some workers are expected to subsidise at least a part of the cost of such training). In Denmark, newcomers are entitled to the equivalent of about 14 months of full-time language study over a three-year period, although most people study for a shorter period than that. In Australia, immigrants are entitled to 510 hours of free language tuition, while refugees and asylum-seekers are offered special preparatory courses in recognition of the particular challenges they may be facing. Some countries also provide occupation-specific courses, which can be of particular value for higher-skilled immigrants working in specialised areas, although resources for such training tend to be limited.

Studies in Scandinavia show that immigrants who take language courses have fewer problems finding work. But they also suggest that there may be a point in language training – at around 500 hours of instruction – when those benefits begin to trail off. The downside of immigrants remaining on in full-time language training is that it prevents them from finding full-time work, which means they're not building up local work experience. And, as we have seen, the lack of such experience is a major barrier to finding work. Indeed, research in Sweden suggests that getting work experience in the first year after arrival has the biggest single impact on longer-term success in the job market, more even than language learning or vocational training.

"The disadvantage of prolonged learning is that it keeps the immigrant away from the labour market.
This is counter-productive in a situation in which employers tend to value work experience in the host country."
Jobs for Immigrants, Volume 1

Mentoring: Settling in a new country can be a disorienting experience. Immigrants face a raft of new challenges, not the least of which is social – getting to know the "locals" and developing a feel for a society's unspoken rules. They also have to figure out how the local jobs scene works – how to write a CV, the best companies to approach, and so on.

One way to help them do all this is to provide a mentor – a local of roughly the same age and who works in the same field. Mentors can help immigrants identify job opportunities, draft CVs, and prepare for interviews. They can also put them in touch with colleagues and friends, and even act as a go-between with a potential employer. The cost to the state of such programmes is low, as mentors are generally unpaid, although they usually receive special training.

Many countries now have mentoring schemes, including Australia and Sweden, although the programmes are usually run locally, and not by the national government. Denmark has experimented with one national scheme – the Kvinfo mentorship programme – which puts immigrant women, especially refugees, in touch with local women. The main aim of the programme is to help the immigrant women to find work, but it also has many other spinoffs, including providing them with valuable social support and an opportunity to practise speaking Danish.

Denmark has come up with other creative ways to help immigrants break the job-market ice. Take Brøndby IF, a professional soccer club near Copenhagen that has about 1 200 amateur players on its books, about a third of whom are from an immigrant background. The club also has an extensive network of about 350 sponsoring firms, and in recent years it has worked to help its members find jobs in those companies. The club's job consultant makes contact with players during training, follows up with interviews to learn more about their skills and interests, and then tries to find a suitable opening in a sponsoring firm. Because training is weekly, it's easy for the consultant to stay in touch with the members; it's easy also for the club's trainers and staff to develop a sense of each jobseeker's personal strengths and weaknesses, which reinforces the confidence of would-be employers in its recommendations.

> **"Employers appear to trust the recommendations of the club, and the responsibility to maintain the reputation of the club is also seen as motivating the young people who receive a job offer to perform well."**
>
> *Jobs for Immigrants, Volume 1*

Recognising qualifications and skills: Many immigrants struggle to get employers to recognise their skills, educational qualifications and previous work experience. Immigrants from outside the OECD area face particular problems, and may find that employers effectively treat them as blank slates, writing off work experience gained overseas.

Many OECD countries have introduced systems to try to improve recognition of qualifications. Australia, which has long favoured skilled immigration, has a well-established and sophisticated system for recognising prior education and skills, however immigrants may still face problems in establishing themselves. For example, people working in self-governing professions like medicine may face a long and complex series of requirements before being allowed to practise. And even where immigrants get the green light for their qualifications, they still face the obstacle that most employers play down the value of overseas work experience.

Some countries have worked to overcome this latter barrier by sponsoring immigrants to go to work in local companies so that they can get work experience but also demonstrate to employers that they have relevant and useful skills. Sweden has introduced a number of such schemes. In one trial scheme, immigrants go to work in a company at no expense to their employer; if the experience doesn't lead to a job, it can still be added to the immigrant's CV as local work experience. In a separate scheme, immigrants are given a three-week apprenticeship within their profession to let them demonstrate that they have the skills to do the job; at the end of the placement they receive a certificate from the workplace to support future job applications.

Discrimination: Just about every developed country has laws outlawing discrimination, both in wider society and in the workplace, and agencies that seek to ensure such legislation is not ignored. Nevertheless, discrimination goes on and affects both immigrants and their descendants, although – as we've seen – determining the scale of it can be difficult. These measurement problems are exacerbated by the reluctance of some countries to ask citizens about their ethnic background, which can make it all but impossible to statistically prove that some groups are sharply underrepresented in the workforce or in certain professions.

The economic and social problems that second and third-generation immigrants are experiencing in many countries, especially Europe, are putting a fresh focus on the need to tackle discrimination. As well as legislation, some countries, including France and the United Kingdom, are experimenting with anonymous CVs, which conceal the identity of job applicants from would-be employers. Many countries are also working to educate employers about the problems immigrants face.

> "The public sector provides the government with a lever to aid labour market integration, as it has a more direct influence on its own employment decisions than those in the private sector."
>
> *International Migration Outlook: SOPEMI 2007*

There have also been limited moves to create "quotas" for immigrants in the public service, which has traditionally been an important job outlet for second-generation immigrants. Belgium has set a target that 4% of public servants should be from an immigrant background, while other countries specify that at least one immigrant – assuming he or she is qualified – should be interviewed for every vacancy in the public service.

Working at the local level

Finally, it's worth considering briefly the level at which state agencies or non-governmental groups can provide support for immigrants – should it all be done by national agencies pursuing nationally set policies, or are there benefits to considering the challenges at the regional or local level?

Migration is often something of a local affair. The influence of things like chain migration and geographical proximity mean immigrants are rarely dispersed equally throughout a country but typically settle in certain cities and towns. Some rural areas, too, may have unusually high levels of immigration, typically where they need to call on large numbers of temporary workers to harvest grapes, for instance. So, across any given country, immigration is usually experienced quite differently between towns, cities and regions.

These variations are important, as they may mean that policies that work well in one place aren't really right for another. And because job markets are also "local" – some regions may have a lot of heavy industry, others may focus on agriculture – there's a double challenge in understanding the interaction of immigrants with employers. In many cases, these complexities are beyond the scope of national policy, and they may best be understood by government operating closer to the local level.

"Local policy makers are able to take into account such variation, along with variation in labour market demand."

From Immigration to Integration

There may be a good case, then, for giving local authorities and officials more room for manoeuvre and a greater degree of autonomy in working with immigrants. This flexibility can also provide room for experimentation, and policies that are shown to work well in one place can be tried out in others.

There's also probably a good case for encouraging a greater role for non-governmental organisations (NGOs), community groups and non-profit bodies, especially where national laws limit the role that government agencies and officials can play with irregular immigrants. Madrid, for instance, has developed an NGO-based system of services for immigrants called CASI. The centres provide everything from emergency housing to help with education, employment and legal problems. The CASI centres, which involve a number of different NGOs, also illustrate the added value that comes from co-ordinating local-level support for immigrants.

Migration and development

Finding a job is one of the keys to immigrants successfully integrating into their new homes. But it can also provide them with the financial means to support families they've left behind, especially in developing countries. In the next chapter, we'll examine the role of such remittances in helping families in developing countries, and the broader issue of whether migration is a plus or a minus for development.

Find Out More

FROM OECD...

On the Internet
To find out more about OECD work on migrants in the labour force, go to *www.oecd.org/els/migration* and follow the links to "migration policies".

Publications
Jobs for Immigrants: Labour Market Integration in Australia, Denmark, Germany and Sweden (2007) and **Jobs for Immigrants: Labour Market Integration in Belgium, France, the Netherlands and portugal** (2008). The first reports from a new series of OECD reviews of the performance of immigrants in individual countries. The aim of the reviews is to determine if programmes and policies in place are effective, and to identify the mix of policies and approaches that help migrants integrate into the labour force, such as language training, programmes for the recognition of qualifications, job-search assistance, and so on.
From Immigration to Integration: Local Solutions to a Global Challenge (2006): Immigration policy is often determined, designed and funded at the national level, but its impact on migrants and society is more strongly felt at the local level where other policies interact. This publication highlights principles and factors which are important in supporting integration locally. A comparison of local initiatives implemented in five OECD countries answers key questions facing all policy makers and stakeholders working in this field. This book provides a set of concrete policy recommendations for implementation at both local and national levels.

Also of interest:
International Migration Outlook: SOPEMI (annual): Includes an update on the job situation of migrants in OECD countries.
The Unemployment Impact of Immigration in OECD Countries (2007) and **Migration in OECD Countries: Labour Market Impact and Integration Issues** (2007): These Working Papers from OECD's Economics department can be found at *www.oecd.org/eco*, and follow the links to "ECO Working Papers".
OECD Economic Surveys: OECD publishes regular Economic Surveys for each member country and for some larger non-members, such as China, Russia and Brazil. Surveys identify the main economic challenges faced by the country and analyse policy options to meet them. To find out more go to *www.oecd.org/eco/surveys*.

... AND OTHER SOURCES
United Nations High Commissioner for Human Rights (*www.ohchr.org*): The ambit of UNHCR includes the protection of migrant workers and their families.
International Labour Organisation (*www.ilo.org*): This UN agency's remit includes promoting decent work for migrants through multilateral actions and policies.

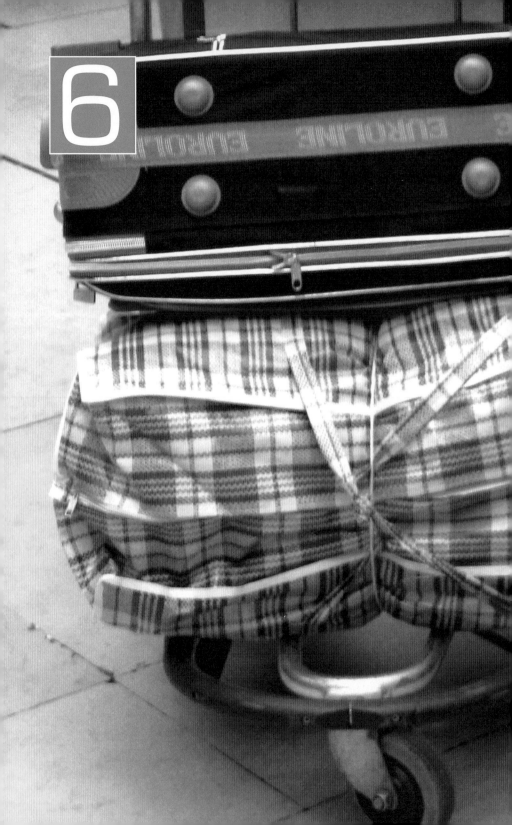

Migration
and Development

For developing countries, migration can be a blessing and a curse:
a blessing for providing remittances and overseas contacts and
experience; a curse for taking away the brightest and the best.
The policy challenge is to minimise the costs and maximise
the benefits for developing and developed countries.

By way of introduction...

The shop sits on the borders of Paris, just a few steps from a Metro station. Outside, a sign announces that it's a travel agency; inside, there are a few phone booths, two Internet stations, and a large desk. Above the desk hangs an aerial photo of the Moroccan city of Fez.

The floor of the shop is filled with luggage – old-fashioned suitcases, unwieldy parcels tied with twine and wrapped in waxed cloth, even a cardboard box that once held a twin baby carriage and is now crammed so full it looks set to burst. The baggage will be taken by truck to Morocco the following week, where it will be picked up by emigrant families back home on vacation, labourers returning home permanently, and the relatives of those still working in France.

Many of the migrants who have left the bags here also regularly send money home – maybe between 50 and 150 euros a month. Some send it through bank orders or agencies like Western Union. Others give it to friends or trusted intermediaries. The money may not sound like much, but in Morocco it can go a long way.

Sitting behind the desk in the shop is Muhammed, who will make sure that these bags and boxes make their way home to Morocco. He admits he's not very happy here in France: "Life here is too expensive, buying power keeps falling, and taxes are very high," he says. "All of this encourages the immigrant to invest his money back home, instead of settling permanently in France..."

▶ Migration helps shape the economic and social direction of some of the world's poorer countries. Sometimes its role is mainly positive, such as when it produces a flood of remittances. But it can also be negative, especially when it steals away the "brightest and best" or deprives families of breadwinners. This chapter examines some of these complex links between migration and development.

Who wins, who loses?

Here's a rule of thumb: Migrants mostly move to countries that are wealthier – albeit sometimes only a little wealthier – than their home countries. This is not to say that migrants only go from poor to rich countries: As Chapter 2 explained, about a third of the world's migrants travel between relatively developed countries, while a third move from developing countries to other developing countries. But it does help to underline the reality that economic factors – the prospects of finding better paid work or a higher standard of living – are important for migrants the world over.

The economic benefits of moving to another country can be substantial in terms of raising the incomes of migrants. But it can also have a powerful impact on the communities they leave behind, especially in the developing world. Some of this impact is positive, such as when remittances help to reduce poverty and allow families to invest in their children's education. But some of it can also be negative, such as when the loss of well educated or highly skilled workers holds back developing countries from reaching their full potential.

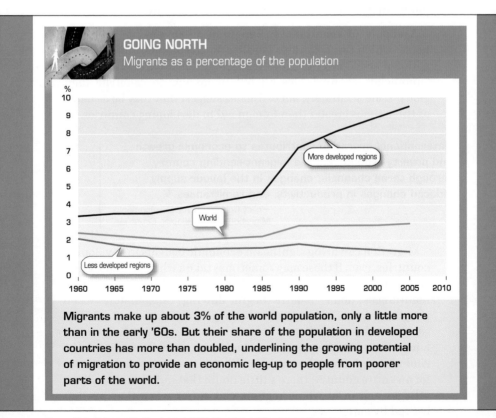

GOING NORTH
Migrants as a percentage of the population

Migrants make up about 3% of the world population, only a little more than in the early '60s. But their share of the population in developed countries has more than doubled, underlining the growing potential of migration to provide an economic leg-up to people from poorer parts of the world.

Source: Policy Coherence for Development 2007: Migration and Development Countries.

StatLink : http://dx.doi.org/10.1787/131678112202

The economic impact of migration on developing countries – both negative and positive – is felt in three main ways:

Changes in the labour force: Depending on how many people are emigrating and who they are, a developing country may find itself short of certain types of workers. In some cases this can lead to a "brain drain", depriving poorer countries of the skilled people needed to kick start their economies and key workers in areas like healthcare and education.

Changes in productivity: Productivity is a measure of the value of the goods and services produced by workers. Generally, more skilled workers have higher levels of productivity – think of the difference between a teenager tossing burgers in a fast-food restaurant and a highly trained chef in a top-class restaurant. In economic terms, a developing country that loses skilled workers may suffer a drop in productivity, which, in turn, will hurt the economy.

A supply of remittances: Emigrants often send money back home, which can help their families, local communities and even national economies. Because many remittances are sent through "unofficial" channels, it's all but impossible to calculate their global scale accurately, but estimates suggest they may be as much as three times greater than foreign aid to developing countries.

"International migration contributes to economic growth and poverty reduction in the migrant-sending country through three channels: changes in the labour supply, induced changes in productivity, and remittances."
Policy Coherence for Development:
Migration and Developing Countries

Migration can bring significant economic benefits to developing countries, even if these may sometimes take a while to materialise, and may only appear at certain stages of migration. For instance, remittances don't usually begin flowing immediately when people emigrate: There's usually a period when they need to get themselves established before they can start sending money home. But there are costs, too, both economically and socially. And although it can be hard to tally up the plusses and minuses for an entire country, there's little doubt that individual families, villages and even whole regions can suffer when they are left behind by emigrants.

Left behind...

It's a strange name for a book – *The Mushroom Covenant*. But for the people of Latvia the subject it covers – emigration and its impact both on those who leave and those who stay – is anything but strange. After their country joined the European Union in 2004, many Latvians took advantage of their newfound freedom to work in some – but not all – of the EU's member states. Britain and Ireland proved popular destinations, and Latvians worked in a number of areas, including mushroom farms, hence the title of book. (More recently, as the economies of western Europe have slowed, there have been signs that emigrants are returning home.)

Latvian families benefit from remittances sent home by emigrants, but they also pay a price. "There is hardly a family left in this country who hasn't lost a son or daughter or mother or father to the mushroom farms of Ireland", Laima Muktupavela, author of *The Mushroom Covenant*, told a reporter. During her time away, she said her four children – "mushroom orphans", as they're known in Latvia – felt abandoned, while her partner left her for a time.

There are similar stories from around the world. Villages where deserted homes stand alongside bright new modern houses built by migrant remittances that may be lived in for no more than a few weeks every year. "In almost every village in rural Mexico you find a kind of ghost town", author Sam Quinones, who has written about the experiences of Mexican emigrants in the United States, told a reporter. "You walk around these gorgeous houses with sliding patio doors and wrought-iron fencing, but no one is around."

> "In Albania, some 20 000 married women were living without their husbands at the time of the 2001 census, while many elderly people have been left behind by their emigrant children, creating the phenomenon of socially-isolated 'elderly orphans'."
>
> Policy Coherence for Development:
> Migration and Developing Countries

Typically, migration – especially when it's temporary or short-term – hollows out the working-age population, leaving children and the elderly behind. Children and young people, of course, may benefit greatly from migrant remittances, particularly when it pays for improved healthcare and education. But their development can suffer when parents go to work overseas. Studies in Bulgaria, which has seen substantial emigration since the end of the communist era, show quite high school-dropout rates among the children of migrants, often because they go to join family members working overseas. Studies in the country also show teachers reporting more discipline problems with students whose parents work overseas.

But the impacts of migration go beyond social concerns in developing countries, affecting economies through the loss of both skilled and unskilled workers...

Brain drains... and gains?

On the Indonesian island of Bali, Yanuar Restu Widodo, a 24-year-old nurse, is making plans for his future. "I could earn $1 500 a month if I work in Japan", the young nurse told a reporter, or about five times more than he earns on Bali. Up to now, Yanuar could only dream, but following a recent agreement between Tokyo and Jakarta to admit 1 000 Indonesian care workers, he can set about turning that idea into reality. "I'll apply as soon as possible," he says.

Japan has traditionally been slow to admit foreign workers, but that may be beginning to change. The agreement with Indonesia marks the first large-scale admission of foreign care workers and nurses. Even though there will be tight restrictions on the Indonesians – they will have to go through special training and exams in Japan – many predict the country's doors will open still further. Japan's population is ageing even more rapidly than in other developed countries, and young people are increasingly unwilling to do "3K jobs" – *kitsui, kitani,* and *kiken,* or difficult, dirty and dangerous.

In future decades, then, nurses from Indonesia and the Philippines could become as familiar sight in Japan as they already are in the rest of the OECD area, where in the year 2000 there were an estimated 110 000 Philippine nurses working. Indeed, anyone who spends time in a hospital in a wealthy country has a pretty good chance of being cared for by a doctor or nurse who was born and trained overseas. The growing role of doctors and nurses from developing countries in OECD countries is much discussed, but what's often less noticed is the effect of their departure – and that of other workers, whether skilled or unskilled – on their home countries. So, what is the impact? The answer depends to some extent on the sort of workers that are leaving, and whether they are low or highly skilled.

When low-skilled workers emigrate...

When low skilled workers depart, the biggest benefit for a developing country may be that their remittances help eat into poverty. There are three main reasons for this:

> Firstly, lower-skilled workers tend to send proportionately more money home in remittances than professionals.

> Secondly, low-skilled workers tend to come from poorer families, so any economic benefits from their departure – for example, remittances – will tend to go to families in greatest need.

> Thirdly, depending on unemployment levels in the home country, the departure of low-skilled workers will either boost the wages of those left behind or create new job opportunities for them.

That last point is worth explaining in a little more detail. Where unemployment is low, companies may find it hard to replace workers who emigrate, so the salaries of people who stay behind will rise as companies hunt around to replace the lost workers, at least in theory. In the real world, however, migration tends to be associated more with joblessness, and there are rarely high levels of emigration from countries where unemployment is low. In this sort of situation, the departure of low-skilled workers can create new opportunities both for people without jobs and for those already in work.

When high-skilled workers emigrate...

On the other hand, the loss of highly skilled and professional workers – the "brain drain" – is often regarded as one of the main dangers of migration, even if the risks are sometimes misrepresented. Indeed, arguments can even be made for some benefits, most notably where there is return migration and people who have gone abroad bring home new skills.

Although it can sometimes sound rather permanent, the reality of international migration is that some people will eventually make their way back home. Even at the height of immigration to the United States at the turn of the 19th and 20th centuries, it's estimated that between a quarter and a third of migrants returned to live in their home countries. Some, indeed, may have travelled repeatedly between the US and their home countries, a phenomenon known as "circular migration".

"Return migration, as well as temporary and circular migration, can promote the circulation and exchange of skills and know-how."

Policy Coherence for Development:
Migration and Developing Countries

The return of migrants – whether permanent or temporary – can bring benefits in many areas. In Mexico, for example, it's been found that children in returnee families are more robust and less likely to die in infancy, which is due in large part to the health knowledge their mothers gained when they were abroad. In economic terms, returnees can bring useful knowledge and contacts from overseas, and can provide an important means for transferring skills.

However, it's important to be realistic about these benefits. The reality is that migrants from wealthier countries are more likely to return home than those from poor and developing countries. Also, migrants may be bringing home newly acquired skills that are not really of use in the developing world.

Understanding the brain drain

One way to understand the scale of the brain drain is to look at the percentage of a country's university graduates who are living overseas. In a list of the 40 countries with the highest proportion of graduates working abroad in OECD countries, a total of 21 of them – just over half – are in Africa, and all but three of those are in sub-Saharan Africa. Unlike, for example, south-eastern Europe, a high number of emigrants from African countries are highly skilled – a phenomenon that leads to losses in three main areas:

➤ Firstly, there's the loss of people who, in normal circumstances, might be expected to be a country's most important innovators and suppliers of new ideas.

➤ Secondly, developing countries "lose" the money they have invested in educating people.

> Thirdly, developing countries may find that shortages of qualified staff make it impossible to deliver adequate healthcare and education.

Perhaps no area of the brain drain has been more discussed than the flow of medical workers around the world. Back in 2000, around 11% of nurses working in the OECD area were foreign born, while for doctors the figure was estimated at 18%. The figures are even higher for individual OECD countries: In the United States around a quarter of doctors were born overseas, in the United Kingdom around a third. In the years since 2000, those numbers have almost certainly risen.

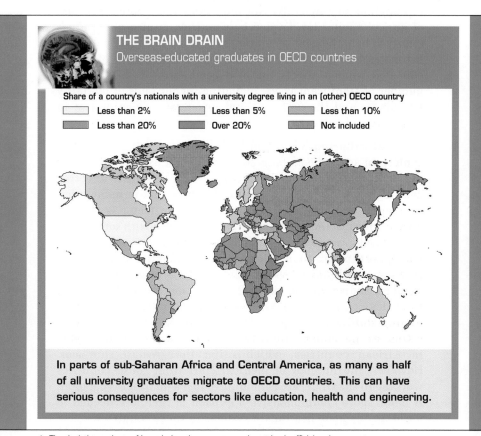

THE BRAIN DRAIN
Overseas-educated graduates in OECD countries

Share of a country's nationals with a university degree living in an (other) OECD country

- Less than 2%
- Less than 5%
- Less than 10%
- Less than 20%
- Over 20%
- Not included

In parts of sub-Saharan Africa and Central America, as many as half of all university graduates migrate to OECD countries. This can have serious consequences for sectors like education, health and engineering.

* The depiction and use of boundaries shown on maps do not imply official endorsement or acceptance by the OECD.

Source: OECD Development Centre.

By sending doctors overseas, taxpayers in poorer countries are in some senses subsidising the medical systems of far wealthier countries. There is also concern that medical schools in developing countries – spurred on by their student's travelling plans – may place too much focus on diseases that are more prevalent in developed countries rather than those found locally. And the brain drain of talented young doctors may also damage poorer countries' abilities to tackle AIDS and HIV.

There's also a gender aspect to the brain drain that is often overlooked. Women in developing countries often face more difficulties than men in going to university. Yet, those women who do make it into third-level education are often highly likely to emigrate subsequently. Not only does that represent a loss of human capital for developing countries, it also undermines efforts to help the next generation to develop to its full potential. Estimates by researchers indicate that the migration of highly educated women affects the next generation of children in a number of significant ways, including higher rates of mortality for infants and the under-5s, and lower rates of enrolment in secondary school.

Overall, the impact of the brain drain is felt particularly acutely in some developing countries, such as Malawi, where the loss of trained medical workers is seriously affecting health care. But it's important to recognise that in many other developing countries, migration is just one factor – and not always the most important one – holding back health services. In some developing countries, the health system can't offer enough job opportunities to medical trainees, making it inevitable that some will look overseas. Also, analysis by United Nations agencies shows that blocking the migration of healthcare staff from developing countries would only go part of the way to easing staffing shortages. The World Health Organisation estimates that about 2.4 million extra medical staff are needed in African countries, which suffer the greatest shortages. However, the number of medical staff from those countries working in the OECD area amounts to just a quarter of that total. A much more comprehensive approach is therefore needed to build up adequate healthcare systems in these countries.

> **"... international migration is neither the main cause, nor would its reduction be the solution to the worldwide health human resources crisis, although it exacerbates the acuteness of the problems in some countries."**
> International Migration Outlook: SOPEMI 2007

A similar point can also be made for developed countries. Too often, overseas medical workers are hired as a quick-fix, when what is really needed is a fundamental rethink of issues like training and the ability of healthcare systems to hold on to qualified staff. Indeed, it's easy to forget that many of the overseas-born medics working in developed countries come from the OECD area themselves. Making better use of locally born health workers will be essential as health systems in OECD countries respond to ageing populations in the years to come.

What is the role of remittances?

Walk around the streets of many of the world's major cities, and you won't travel too far before encountering the familiar golden "M" of a McDonald's or the distinctive mermaid logo of a Starbucks. These food outlets seem singularly ubiquitous, but there's another American-owned business that has even more international outposts. In fact, it has more than McDonald's, Starbucks, Burger King and Wal-Mart combined – five times more, according to the *New York Times*. What is it? Western Union.

What are remittances?

In simple terms, remittances can be thought of as money migrants send back to their home countries, usually for the use of their families or – eventually – themselves. Migrants may also build up savings when they're overseas, and if they then return home permanently and bring this money with them it's also generally considered a remittance.

From the point of view of compiling statistics, the definition can be even broader, and may include all money paid to temporary migrants when they're overseas or to workers who commute across an international border, such as Belgians who work in Luxembourg.

WHO GETS WHAT?
Remittances as a percentage of GDP, 2006

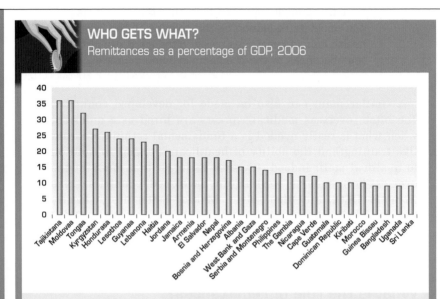

This graphic shows the value of money sent home by migrants to remitance-receiving countries as a percentage of their GDP. For example, in Tajikistan in 2006, remittances accounted for 36%, of GDP – equivalent, in effect, to more than a third of the country's total economic activity.

However, this is just one way of measuring the scale of remittances.

For instance, one could also look at remittances in terms of the actual money received by each country (data which also have the advantage of being more up to date).

In 2007, the top 10 remittance-receiving countries were estimated as follows by the World Bank:

India	$27.0 billion	Spain	$8.9 billion
China	$25.7 billion	Belgium	$7.2 billion
Mexico	$25.0 billion	Germany	$7.0 billion
Philippines	$17.0 billion	United Kingdom	$7.0 billion
France	$12.5 billion	Romania	$6.8 billion

The presence of wealthy OECD European countries on this list may seem surprising. In reality, a great deal of the money that goes to these countries is not remittances as they are popularly understood. For example, salaries paid to people living in one country but working in another – such as Belgians who commute to work in Luxembourg every day – are regarded from a statistical point of view as remittances.

Source: World Bank (2008), Migration and Remittances Factbook 2008.

The company began life in the 1850s to send telegraphs across the vast North American continent, and then came close to collapse at the dawn of the age of the Internet era. But in recent years it has reinvented itself by focusing on one particular business – transmitting migrants' remittances. The activities of Western Union may sometimes be controversial – critics have accused it of charging excessive fees – but its success is a mark of the huge growth in migrant remittances.

In 1995, the value of remittances worldwide was put at $102 billion; by 2005, that had more than doubled to an estimated $232 billion, well in excess of what was given in overseas development aid or foreign direct investment. By 2007, the figure had reached $318 billion, according to World Bank estimates, of which $240 billion, or about 75%, went to developing countries. And, because a substantial slice of remittances goes through "unofficial channels" – in other words, not through banks or agencies like Western Union – the actual figures are almost certainly considerably higher than these estimates.

Who remits and why?

What determines how much money migrants send? It's hardly surprising that migrants who leave a spouse and children behind tend to send more home than people who travel with their families. It's not unusual for solo migrants to also be lower skilled workers, which, in turn, usually means they come from poorer communities.

> "… Migrants' intention to return to their family is a key factor in motivating high savings and remittances."
>
> Policy Coherence for Development:
> Migration and Developing Countries

The impact of these factors are clearly visible in global remittance patterns. For example, the many millions of migrants working in the Persian Gulf region send home more money per head – over $2 600 a year – than migrants anywhere else in the world. Most of these migrant are low-skilled labourers from Asian countries, such as Bangladesh and the Philippines, and most will eventually go back home. In the meantime, the money they send back to their families can be hard-earned. The United States government, for instance, has spoken of "conditions of involuntary servitude" in the Gulf state of Qatar, as well as workers who are offered misleading contract terms when they are recruited and who "often suffer miserable working and living conditions".

Other factors also affect the scale of remittances. For example, the longer emigrants spend away, the smaller the share of their income they tend to send home, although it may take some years before this effect becomes noticeable. This fall off may also be balanced by the tendency of migrants' incomes to rise over time, so their remittances may not decline in real terms but only as a proportion of their overall earnings.

Why do emigrants send money home? One Nigerian emigrant in London replied that "it is my social, moral, cultural duty to help the family" when asked that question by a reporter. No doubt that sums up the thinking of many migrants, but buried

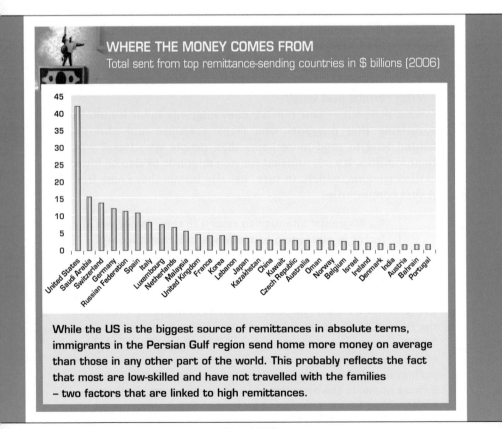

WHERE THE MONEY COMES FROM
Total sent from top remittance-sending countries in $ billions (2006)

While the **US** is the biggest source of remittances in absolute terms, immigrants in the Persian Gulf region send home more money on average than those in any other part of the world. This probably reflects the fact that most are low-skilled and have not travelled with the families – two factors that are linked to high remittances.

Source: World Bank (2008), Migration and Remittances Factbook 2008.

in such responses are a whole range of motivations for sending remittances that are worth exploring in a little more detail.

> **"The studies that analyse this phenomenon [of remittances] provide useful descriptive evidence and results from empirical research, but they only explain it partly..."**
> International Migration Outlook: SOPEMI 2006

Overall, there is no general theory to explain migrant remittances, but experts who have studied this question have proposed a series of "models" that attempt to explain why migrants send money home. These include "pure altruism", where the motivation is simply that migrants want to help their families, and at the other end of the scale, "pure self-interest", where the motivation is to encourage relatives to care for assets left behind, like a farm or a car, or to build up status in their community.

There are more complex explanations, too, such as "implicit family agreement", where remittances are seen as a payback to the family for paying the migrant's fare and providing support during the first few months away. Migrants may also "pay back" what they feel they owe to their families by supporting the next generation in their attempts to emigrate. Finally, remittances are

---

MIGRATION IN A RECESSION   Remittances

Remittances to developing countries started slowing in late 2008 as the global economic slowdown began to bite, the World Bank estimates. In the previous year, their value had been equivalent to 2% of the GDP of developing countries, but the World Bank reckoned this would fall to 1.8% in 2008 and to about 1.6% in 2009. These falls are not insignificant, but they need to be seen in context. Firstly, not every developing country will be affected equally. Secondly, other income flows – such as overseas aid and foreign investment – will also slow in the slump, leading remittances to account for an even bigger share of inflows to developing countries.

Historically, indeed, remittances have tended to prove fairly resilient during slowdowns for several reasons:
Firsly, emigrant communities build up over many years and don't simply vanish at the first hint of recession.
Secondly, if emigrants do decide to return home, they will usually bring savings with them, which count as remittances.
And, thirdly, remittances account for only one part of each emigrant's outgoings; even if their income falls, emigrants have traditionally made other sacrifices to try to go on sending money back home.

---

sometimes also explained in terms of "migrant savings targets", which assume that migrants have the goal of going home with certain sums in savings; their ability to reach those goals will depend on how much they're earning, their day-to-day costs, and family demands for support.

> **"... it may be the case that remittances are driven by all of these motives at the same time, each one explaining a part of the remittance amount or period of remitting practice."**
>
> International Migration Outlook: SOPEMI 2006

None of these concepts offers a perfect method for predicting how much migrants will send home, and they also tend to exclude the potential importance of other factors – such as political and economic stability in the home country or the existence of financial incentives for migrants to send home income. In reality, remittances are probably driven by a mix of all these motivations, which rise and fall in their significance at various times.

How are remittances made?

The ways in which migrants send money home depends on a mix of what transfer means are available to them, what's safest, what's quickest and what's cheapest. Their options traditionally range from the informal – for example, simply putting it in their pockets and jumping on a boat or a plane that's heading back home – to formal channels, such as bank transfers.

At the informal end of the spectrum, probably the simplest method is hand-carrying money, which can be done by the migrant or a trusted friend or relative. For a long time it was thought only small numbers of quite poor migrants used this method, but research indicates it may be more widespread. According to some estimates, hand-carrying may account for 10% of remittances by Latin American migrants in the United States, and as much as 50% of remittances by Romanians.

Many Asian migrants rely on informal systems in which their money is never physically or electronically transferred. These systems – known variously as *hawala, hundi* or *fei ch'ien* (literally, "flying money") – are based on intermediaries and trust. A typical transfer might work like this: A Pakistani migrant in London goes to a trusted *hawalader*, or intermediary, and hands over the money he wants to transfer. The *hawalader* then contacts a counterpart in Pakistan, and asks him to pay over the sum of money to the migrant's family. Although the Pakistan *hawalader* has paid out on this deal and received nothing in return, chances are that there will be other deals where he will gain money in transfers from Pakistan to London. Where the payments to and fro don't cancel each other out, the *hawaladers* organise an annual settling of accounts to balance the books. This relationship between the *hawaladers* relies on trust – and fear of the consequences if anyone tries to cheat.

Migrants also have a wide range of more formal transfer options, ranging from immigrant-run businesses – known as "ethnic stores" in the United States, to post offices, transfer giants like Western Union and Money Gram, as well as banks. And, in the future, it's likely that migrants will be make increasing use of mobile phone technologies to transfer money, which are being pioneered by the likes of CitiBank, MasterCard, Western Union and Vodaphone.

Such approaches may help cut the costs of a making transfers through formal channels, which is a serious burden for many migrants. According to estimates by the Inter American Development Bank, a migrant sending $200 back home will pay an agency like Western Union as much as $24 in commission, or 12%, and around $14, or 7%, to a bank. By contrast, the commission on a *hawala* transfer is usually under 2%. Indeed, the development bank estimated that the total cost of sending remittances to the Caribbean and Latin America in 2002 was $4 billion, or about one-eighth of what migrants from that region sent back home that year.

> " ... if immigrants who regularly dispatch most of their disposable income in remittances could acquire the habit of accumulating money in a bank account, they would attain benefits that go beyond economising on the costs of remittance."
>
> Migration, Remittances and Development

Why does this matter? Firstly, the payment of a $24 commission on a $200 remittance amounts to a considerable loss of potential spending power for both the migrant and her family, even if the method of payment brings extra security and peace of mind. Secondly, relying on international transfer agencies, and more informal systems, deprives migrants of some of the benefits of getting a foothold in the financial system by opening a bank account. As well as the potential for lower transfer fees if they're customers, migrants could also potentially take out cheaper loans than if they're depending on neighbourhood loan sharks, and – in some countries – take advantage of low-tax retirement and savings accounts.

Many migrants, however, can find banks unapproachable, especially if they're struggling to learn the language of their adopted country, while irregular migrants may be unable to open accounts if they don't have a social security number or ID card. In response, some countries are moving to make bank transfers easier for migrants, even those without legal status. In the United States, the Federal Reserve, or central bank, has established the "Directo a Mexico" programme that allows all Mexicans living in the United States, regardless of status, to send money back home for no more than a few dollars per transfer. Opponents accuse the programme of undermining United States migration laws, but supporters say that keeping money transfers in the open may help to combat the crime that's sometimes associated with informal transfer systems.

What is the impact of remittances?

Wander into a village in a developing country like the Philippines, and the impact of remittances on families soon becomes apparent. Homes with a son or daughter or father or mother working overseas may be putting up a new roof or even building a new house, there may be a colour TV blaring out the latest episode of a soap opera, the kids may be wearing brightly coloured clothes sent home in big bundles from places like Hong Kong or Singapore, and when it comes to mealtimes there may be more food on the table – rice and local meat and vegetables, but also treats like imported candy bars.

For families and villages – the micro level – the impact of remittances can be quite considerable, but at the regional or national level – the macro level – their impact is less clear. Remittances may reduce poverty, but can they also increase inequality? And if remittances generate local economic activity, such as house building, can they also affect national economic growth and, if so, how?

One of the clearest impacts of remittances is in reducing poverty or, more precisely, absolute poverty – essentially, people living on under a dollar a day (see box). According to researchers at the World Bank, a 10% increase in remittances per person to a

---

How is poverty defined?

There are many different ways to measure poverty, but two of the most important are in terms of whether it is absolute or relative. **Absolute poverty** generally refers to people who are surviving on less than a certain fixed sum of money, usually a dollar a day.

Relative poverty is a more fluid concept, and describes whether people are poor compared with other people in their country or community.

---

developing country decreases absolute poverty by 3.5%. Arguably, this improvement understates the impact of remittances: Even though some families will remain below the poverty line, they will still see some improvement in their income as a result of remittances – indeed, for the poorest families, remittances can account for a very large percentage of their income.

Remittances may also have an impact on income inequality, in other words, the gap between the poor and better off. The usual measure of income inequality is the Gini index, where 0 equals absolute equality and 1 absolute inequality. (Such places don't exist in the real world, but in a country with a Gini coefficient of 0, everybody would have exactly the same income; in a country with a coefficient of 1, just one person would have all the income, and everyone else would have nothing.)

The research findings from around the world are mixed – in some countries, such as Tonga and Mexico, remittances seem to have decreased income inequality. In others, such as Egypt, they increased it. This may be because families that are relatively better off can more easily afford the initial costs of sending off a son or daughter to work overseas than their poorer counterparts, and so are more likely ultimately to benefit from remittances. Some researchers argue that in countries where income inequality is relatively low to start with, remittances will tend to lower it still further; but, where income inequality is high, remittances may only make it worse.

What are remittances spent on? There's no simple answer to this question – situations vary greatly, not just from family to family but also country to country. But for a range of reasons, it's relatively unusual for families receiving remittances to invest directly in the economy by, for instance, opening businesses. Instead, much of the money tends to go on typical day-to-day expenditures, like food and clothing, especially among poorer families. Typically, remittances are also devoted to children's education, paying off debts, paying for healthcare, buying land and building houses. A share, also, may go on luxuries, some of which are likely to be imported, meaning that money sent back to the home country may soon leave it.

Some overseas migrant groups have sought ways to make remittances more effective for the entire community back home, and not just individual families. Beginning in the 1960s, emigrants from the Mexican state of Zacatecas in the United States began forming home-town associations to help each other out if they fell ill and to organise the return of bodies of the deceased. These *Clubes Zacatecanos* eventually broadened their role, and supported projects back home, such as repairs to churches and plazas. Their efforts later received official backing, with the state government matching each dollar collectively remitted by the clubs under a scheme called 2x1. Today, 3x1 programmes operate across Mexico at the federal level, with government providing two dollars for every dollar of collective remittance. Much of the money is used to fund water and sewage projects, community development centres and school scholarships. The success of such schemes highlights the potential for diaspora networks and hometown associations to support development back home, and this can go beyond financial aid: Emigrants can also provide their home communities with much-needed expertise and skills and provide valuable business and social contacts.

Whatever way they're delivered – individually or collectively – remittances can have a significant economic impact, mainly through what economists call the "multiplier" effect. Think of it this way: A family building a new house will have to hire a builder; he, in turn, will probably have to hire a couple of helpers and buy building supplies; the building supplier, meanwhile, may find that he's so busy he now has to hire some new staff or buy a computer, which means extra business for the computer store, and so on... This chain of consequences is so significant that researchers have even set out to measure it. In Mexico, for instance, it's been estimated that every dollar in remittance, or "migradollar", received by families in cities leads to an increase in GNP of $2.90. (GNP – or gross national product – is a widely used measure for economic activity that occurs solely within a country's borders.)

By supplying foreign currency, remittances have other economic benefits. They can ease deficits in the balance of payments accounts, which represent money flowing into a country versus money flowing out. The economics is complicated but, in simple terms, remittances represent a positive contribution to the balance of payments, which is why some developing countries over the years have actively encouraged migrants to send money home.

That's all to the economic good, but there may be potential downsides, too. Some analysts argue that remittances create a dependency culture – leaving people reliant on handouts and unwilling to take risks or even to do much in the way of actual work. There may also be direct and unwanted economic changes, which economists sometimes group under the heading "Dutch disease".

The term was inspired by the experience of the Netherlands in the 1960s, when it suddenly discovered large deposits of natural gas in the North Sea. Good news, but the Netherlands' new-found wealth had an unwelcome side effect: The value of its currency began rising against other currencies, which made Dutch exports more expensive and less competitive overseas and left the manufacturing sector struggling. A windfall of remittances – like the discovery of natural gas – can have a similar impact: The currency's value may begin to rise and the economy may focus on satisfying local needs (such as building houses), shifting energy away from manufacturing and making what exports are produced more expensive.

> **"… remittances are not a panacea, and cannot substitute for sound economic policies in developing countries."**
> Migration, Remittances and Development

To be fair, evidence of remittances having such an impact is relatively slim. Equally, however, there is no clinching argument for saying that large-scale remittances will always fuel economic growth. Situations vary from country to country, and the benefits of remittances can easily be lost in the absence of well thought-out development policies.

Final thoughts...

Of course, development is only aspect of international migration. As this book has shown repeatedly, governments face challenges in a wide range of areas to maximise the benefits and minimise the drawbacks of migration. In the next, and final, chapter of this book we'll review some of the issues this book has looked at, and take a look at the some of the statistical issues involved in measuring international migration.

Find Out More

FROM OECD...

On the Internet

For an introduction to OECD work on development and migration visit *www.oecd.org/dev/migration*.

Publications

Policy Coherence for Development 2007: Migration and Developing Countries (2007): This report examines the costs and benefits of migration for developing countries, and looks at ways migration flows could be better managed around the world. The report encourages receiving countries to look at migration policies through a development lens and sending countries to look at development policies through a migration lens. Interlinking migration and development policies promises a more effective pursuit of the objectives of both sets of policies. This volume provides the basis for a productive debate surrounding policy innovations maximising the overall benefits of international migration.

Gaining from Migration: Towards a New Mobility System (2007): How should the global system of labour mobility be managed to better meet the needs of sending countries, receiving countries, and migrants themselves? In short, how can we all gain more from migration? This report is a summary of recommendations that seek to answer this question. New ideas, based on an exhaustive review of past policy experiences in Europe and elsewhere, are offered for policies related to labour markets, integration, development co-operation and the engagement of diasporas.

... AND OTHER SOURCES

Global Forum On Migration and Development (*www.gfmd-fmmd.org*): An informal and state-led global forum that seeks to provide "a platform for policymakers to share information on ideas, good practices and policies regarding migration and development, and to explore new initiatives for international cooperation...".

United Nations Development Programme (*www.undp.org/poverty/migration. htm*): This UN agency works on migration "because of the many impacts it can have on poor people and poor countries".

World Bank (*www.worldbank.org*): The Bank's work includes assessing the scale of international remittances and the impact of payment systems. Its website includes a special section on remittances: *www.worldbank.org/remittances*.

International Monetary Fund (*www.imf.org*): The IMF does work on the impact of international migration in the context of economic globalisation and on assessing the scale of remittances. Search for "migration" or "remittances" at the IMF Web site.

Institute for the Study of International Migration (*www12.georgetown.edu/sfs/isim*): Based at Georgetown University, ISIM hosts a special research consortium on the role of remittances in situations of conflict and crisis.

7

Its pace has varied throughout the ages, but our journey around
our planet has been – and will remain – a constant in human
history. Responding to this evolving phenomenon is vital if societies
are to continue to gain benefits from international migration.
Plus, an introduction to measuring migration.

By Way of
Conclusion…

The journey goes on...

The future is rarely clear, but there are at least a few things that can be predicted with some certainty. One of these is that migration will go on. The journey that began millennia ago on the plains of Africa is still continuing, and will go on for as long as humans call this planet home.

What is less clear, of course, are the paths that this journey will take and the identity of the travellers. In other words, who will tomorrow's migrants be, where will they come from and where will they want to go? Equally important, what sort of welcome will they get?

The answers to these questions will vary greatly from country to country, and they will also vary over time. International migration can change surprisingly quickly. Take Ireland: In the 150 years after the end of the potato famines in the mid-19th century, around 5 million people left Ireland – a figure higher than the country's population today. But in the mid-1990s, as its economy boomed, Ireland went from being a country of emigration to one of immigration. Today, around 14% of people living in Ireland were born outside the country, an astonishing turnaround that has happened in less than a generation.

A sizeable number of these new Irish have come from a country at the other end of Europe, Poland. Since it joined the European Union in 2004, many Poles have gone to work in other EU countries, including the United Kingdom, Ireland and Germany. In the United Kingdom alone, for example, almost 160 000 Poles registered to work in 2006, more than double the number in 2004. But as Poland's economy has picked up in recent years and those of the United Kingdom and Ireland have slowed, there are signs that many are returning home again. Some argue that migration within the European Union area – and more broadly – will increasingly come to resemble a system of international labour mobility, with workers flying on budget airlines to where they can find jobs, but keeping in touch with work opportunities back home *via* the Internet.

Governments and countries – both in countries of emigration and of immigration – can struggle to keep up with these changes, and today's policies may not match tomorrow's realities. The task becomes still harder if the lessons of the past and the present are ignored. If international migration shows one thing, it's that there is a lot to be learnt both from the experiences of the past and of other countries – and a high price to be paid for failing to respond to changing situations. Working with countries to share and to learn from these experiences is a major part of the OECD's mission.

> "... the international mobility of people needs to be well managed, and sound policies designed and implemented."
>
> Angel Gurría, OECD Secretary-General
> (speech in Paris, June 2007)

Challenges and opportunities...

As this book has attempted to show, migration is both an opportunity and a challenge for OECD countries. Population ageing will lead to more demand, especially from business, for immigration. But, of course, immigration can only be a partial response, and wider changes will be needed, including improved training and education for locals in the workforce and – in all likelihood – later retirement ages.

There are other obstacles, too. In most developed countries the levels of immigration that would be needed to compensate for population ageing would be unacceptable to the bulk of voters. Indeed, even existing levels of migration often face considerable public resistance, and this is only likely to grow in the midst of a global economic slowdown. The situation also isn't helped by the persistence of irregular immigration. Even if its extent and its impacts are often overstated, the existence of irregular immigration tends to add fuel to the anti-immigrant fires, helping to cool the welcome for those with a legitimate right to enter and stay.

> "The better targeted integration policies are, the more successful integration will be. This in turn will greatly reduce the risk of political backlash against immigrants."
>
> Angel Gurría, OECD Secretary-General
> (speech in Paris, February 2008)

That's a pity, as immigrants have repeatedly demonstrated that they are a vital force in our societies. In business, think of the contribution of the thousands of immigrants who quietly run corner shops in cities around the world, or of those who have achieved outstanding success – Belgian-born Liz Claiborne became a fashion icon in New York, while on America's West Coast, Germany's Andreas von Bechtolsheim and India's Vinod Khosla co-founded Sun Microsystems and China's Charles Wang founded Computer Associates. In the arts, Sweden's Claes Oldenburg and the Netherlands' Willem De Kooning became leading figures in the United States, which was also where Canadian singer-songwriters Joni Mitchell, Alanis Morissette and Leonard Cohen made their names; on both sides of the Atlantic, some of the most important figures in modern writing were born overseas – leading "British" writers include Salman Rushdie (born in Mumbai), Monica Ali (born in Dhaka) and Lucy Ellman (born in Illinois), to name just a few, while Canada is home to another famous Indian immigrant writer, Rohinton Mistry.

The list of achievements goes on and on... and yet despite such success stories, there is little doubt that in many countries international migration has something of an image problem. In part that's based on problems newcomers in some countries have faced in areas like employment and education, never mind more contentious issues such as the extent of their cultural assimilation.

Results from PISA show many young immigrants are facing problems in education, and aren't keeping up with their native counterparts. Failure to tackle these risks will deprive young immigrants – first, second and subsequent generations – of the chance to develop their talents and abilities, and the capacity to support themselves in later life.

Equally, in the workforce, many immigrants are not doing as well as their education and training might suggest. That's a loss to them, but it's also a loss to the societies they live in, which are failing to make the most of these immigrants' human capital. Already, many governments have introduced policies to try to address these issues, including language programmes, systems for recognising overseas qualifications, and support for immigrants to spend time with local companies so that they can learn how the workplace operates in their adopted countries and also demonstrate their own skills. Undoubtedly, though, much more will need to be done.

As we've seen, migration doesn't affect only immigrants and the countries they come to live in. It can also have a big impact on the families, communities and countries they leave behind, especially in the developing world. The impact can be beneficial, through remittances, but also detrimental, such as when a brain drain of trained staff causes shortages in crucial areas like healthcare and education. There is a responsibility on governments both in developed and developing countries to find ways to maximise these benefits and minimise the drawbacks.

A better debate

Complex, contentious, controversial – international migration can sometimes be seen as the third rail of political life, a spot that offers only risks and no rewards to policy makers as they try to balance the positives with the negatives. Too often also, public debate on the issue is hijacked by hysteria, with reality obscured by myths, and complexity by generalisations.

> **"To be prepared for the future, governments need to act now to put proper policies in place to help satisfy labour needs partly through migration and to enable the integration of migrants. Every OECD country should make this a priority. It is socially, politically, ethically, and morally correct, but it is also an act of sheer economic rationality."**
>
> Angel Gurría, OECD Secretary-General
> (speech in Paris, February 2008)

We owe it to ourselves and to the people who come to live amongst us to have a more reasoned migration debate – a better debate, one informed by facts, not fancy. Without such a debate, we risk missing out on the many benefits of immigration, and repeating the errors of yesterday. Without such a debate, we will fail to design the policies needed for the migration of tomorrow – not just in how we manage migration, but in how we configure our societies, our schools, our workplaces to ensure that those who travel and those who stay home reap the full benefits of our continuing human journey.

Some statistics

One of OECD's major contributions to understanding migration is the work it does on gathering and compiling international data on migration flows as well as on the size of migrant populations and their characteristics, such as age, gender, educational qualification and occupations. This data allows international comparisons to be made regarding the state of migration in various OECD countries. It also helps policy makers and planners to better understand the challenges and opportunities arising from international migration.

This book has already made extensive use of this data, albeit in a somewhat simplified form. This final section offers a more detailed introduction to OECD's work on the measurement of international migration, and explains some of the challenges facing statisticians in gathering this data.

Definitions for internationally comparable data

Compiling internationally comparable data on migration is a challenge for many reasons, not the least of which is that governments don't always compile comprehensive and specific data both on migration flows – movements in and out of the country – and on the size of foreign-born populations. It's true that some countries do assemble data in some of these areas, but for others the numbers must sometimes be inferred from data sources such as population registers or from registration and work permits.

However, the rules governing such registration and permit systems vary greatly, making international comparisons difficult. For example, in some countries people staying for just three months are required to register themselves; in others, they can stay for up to 12 months without registering. So, statisticians who want to measure differences in migration between countries need to take account of such variations. But there are challenges for statisticians even when they're working with specific data on migrants. Countries often use different statistical definitions to compile such numbers; for example, some count seasonal workers as immigrants, others do not.

While standardised international data on migration flows would be a benefit for planners and international agencies, countries are naturally free to make their own decisions on how much data to collect and how to do so. Data collection can be an expensive business, and it can touch on other issues, too, such as people's right to privacy.

Nevertheless, over the years some attempts have been made, most notably by the United Nations, to improve the comparability of international data by developing a coherent framework for international migration statistics. In simple terms, the UN speaks of a long-term migrant as someone who moves from their "country of usual residence" for more than a year, and a short-term migrant as someone who moves for more than three but fewer than twelve months. There are a number of international initiatives going on to encourage countries to adopt and use these definitions, but progress has been slow. As a result, it's currently very difficult to compile internationally comparable data based on these definitions, although that may well change in the years to come.

In the interim, OECD has adopted its own definitions, which echo those of the UN by emphasising the distinction between short and long-term, or temporary and permanent, immigration. An immigrant is thus defined as "a person of foreign nationality who enters the permanently resident population either from outside the country or by changing from a temporary to a permanent status in the country".

The justification for this definition is that just about every country distinguishes between temporary and permanent immigration or, in effect, people who are staying only for a while and those who expect to stay "for good" (even if in reality some of these will eventually go back home and some may move on to another country). The complication is that this distinction between temporary and permanent isn't always reflected in the sorts of permits given to immigrants. For instance, in many European countries permanent-type immigrants may be given permits that last for just a year. However, these permits may be indefinitely renewable, meaning that the immigrant is effectively on a permanent track.

Because the distinction between temporary and permanent is widely understood and can be investigated in most countries through formal migration data or through population or labour data, it provides a basis for creating internationally comparable statistics on international migration. It's worth noting, that this "standardised" data can be very different from official national data produced by OECD countries. This is not to say that such national data are wrong; it's just based on different definitions. For example, many countries count international students as migrants; for the sake of creating internationally comparable statistics, the OECD doesn't.

Inflows and outflows of migrants ("flows")

As we've seen, OECD countries don't always directly measure arrivals and exits of foreigners, so data on such inflows and outflows has to be gathered in other ways, usually through population registers, or residence permit data or statistical surveys. Each of these data sources has its own particular characteristics.

Data from population registers: Many, but not all, countries expect residents – whether native or foreign-born – to register themselves, although the length of time that people intend to reside before they have to register can vary greatly, typically from between three to twelve months, which creates problems for drawing up internationally comparable statistics. Registers also tend to be better at recording inflows than outflows, as people planning to emigrate may not bother to remove their name from the register.

Data from residence and work permits: Many countries issue immigrants with permits that allow them residence or the right to work, however such data isn't always a comprehensive indicator of migrant inflows. For example, people living in free-movement areas, such as much of the European Union zone, are not always required to seek a permit. And even where permits are required, issued permits may not always be used. For example, people seeking to immigrate may apply for a permit from overseas and then decide not to travel. Finally, permits may sometimes be granted to people who are already living in a country, either as a renewal of an earlier permit or to mark a change of status.

Data from surveys: Data for a number of countries are compiled from surveys. For example, the United Kingdom's International Passenger Survey samples roughly one in every 500 passengers entering or leaving the country on aeroplanes, trains and boats.

The following two tables show inflows (**Table 1**) and outflows (**Table 2**) from a number of OECD countries over a 10-year period, and indicate the main source of data for each country.

TABLE 1. INFLOWS OF FOREIGN POPULATION INTO SELECTED OECD COUNTRIES
Thousands

	1997	1998	1999	2000	2001	2002	2003	2004	2005	2006
Inflow data based on population registers:										
Austria	..	59.2	72.4	66.0	74.8	92.6	97.2	108.9	101.5	85.4
Belgium	49.2	50.7	57.8	57.3	66.0	70.2	68.8	72.4	77.4	83.4
Czech Republic	9.9	7.9	6.8	4.2	11.3	43.6	57.4	50.8	58.6	66.1
Denmark	20.4	21.3	20.3	22.9	25.2	22.0	18.7	18.8	20.1	23.0
Finland	8.1	8.3	7.9	9.1	11.0	10.0	9.4	11.5	12.7	13.9
Germany	615.3	605.5	673.9	648.8	685.3	658.3	601.8	602.2	579.3	558.5
Hungary	13.3	16.1	20.2	20.2	20.3	18.0	19.4	22.2	25.6	19.4
Japan	274.8	265.5	281.9	345.8	351.2	343.8	373.9	372.0	372.3	325.6
Luxembourg	9.4	10.6	11.8	10.8	11.1	11.0	12.6	12.2	13.8	13.7
Netherlands	76.7	81.7	78.4	91.4	94.5	86.6	73.6	65.1	63.4	67.7
Norway	22.0	26.7	32.2	27.8	25.4	30.8	26.8	27.9	31.4	37.4
Slovak Republic	6.1	6.4	5.9	4.6	4.7	4.8	4.6	7.9	7.7	11.3
Spain	35.6	57.2	99.1	330.9	394.0	443.1	429.5	645.8	682.7	803.0
Sweden	33.4	35.7	34.6	42.6	44.1	47.6	48.0	47.6	51.3	80.4
Switzerland	72.8	74.9	85.8	87.4	101.4	101.9	94.0	96.3	94.4	102.7
Inflow data based on residence permits or on other sources:										
Australia										
Permanent inflows	*104.6*	*94.2*	*101.0*	*111.3*	*131.2*	*121.2*	*125.9*	*150.0*	*167.3*	*179.8*
Temporary inflows	147.1	173.2	194.1	224.0	245.1	240.5	244.7	261.6	289.4	321.6
Canada										
Permanent inflows	216.0	174.2	190.0	227.5	250.6	229.0	221.4	235.8	262.2	251.6
Temporary inflows	194.4	198.4	232.8	260.9	282.0	262.0	243.3	244.3	246.7	268.1
France	74.5	110.7	82.8	91.9	106.9	124.3	136.4	141.6	135.9	135.1
Greece	..	38.2	..	..	..	..	..	..	..	..
Ireland	23.7	21.7	22.2	27.8	32.7	39.9	42.4	41.8	66.1	88.9
Italy	..	111.0	268.0	271.5	232.8	388.1	..	319.3	206.8	181.5
Korea	..	..	..	185.4	172.5	170.9	178.3	188.8	266.3	314.7
Mexico	27.1	25.3	22.7	24.2	26.1	24.6	29.1	34.0	39.3	47.6
New Zealand	32.9	27.4	31.0	37.6	54.4	47.5	43.0	36.2	54.1	49.8
Poland	..	5.2	17.3	15.9	21.5	30.2	30.3	36.9	38.5	34.2
Portugal	3.3	6.5	10.5	15.9	151.4	72.0	31.8	34.1	28.1	42.2
Turkey	128.5	143.0	154.3	162.3	154.9	151.8	147.2	148.0	169.7	191.0
United Kingdom	237.2	287.3	337.4	379.3	373.3	418.2	406.8	494.1	473.8	509.8
United States										
Permanent inflows	797.8	653.2	644.8	841.0	1 058.9	1 059.4	703.5	957.9	1 122.4	1 266.3
Temporary inflows	999.6	997.3	1 106.6	1 249.4	1 375.1	1 282.6	1 233.4	1 299.3	1 323.5	1 457.9

Source: International Migration Outlook: SOPEMI 2008.

StatLink ᵐᵖ⧉ : *http://dx.doi.org/10.1787/430155301562*

TABLE 2. OUTFLOWS OF FOREIGN POPULATION FROM SELECTED OECD COUNTRIES
Thousands

	1997	1998	1999	2000	2001	2002	2003	2004	2005	2006
Outflow data based on population registers:										
Austria	..	44.9	47.3	44.4	51.0	38.8	46.1	48.3	47.5	52.9
Belgium	34.6	36.3	36.4	35.6	31.4	31.0	33.9	37.7	38.5	39.4
Czech Republic	0.1	0.2	0.1	0.2	20.6	31.1	33.2	33.8	21.8	31.4
Denmark	6.7	7.7	8.2	8.3	8.9	8.7	8.7	9.4	9.4	9.8
Finland	1.6	1.7	2.0	4.1	2.2	2.8	2.3	4.2	2.6	2.7
Germany	637.1	639.0	555.6	562.4	497.0	505.6	499.1	547.0	483.6	483.8
Hungary	1.9	2.3	2.5	2.2	1.9	2.4	2.6	3.5	3.3	3.2
Japan	177.8	188.1	199.7	210.9	232.8	248.4	259.4	278.5	292.0	218.8
Luxembourg	5.8	6.7	6.9	7.1	7.8	8.3	6.9	7.5	7.2	7.7
Netherlands	21.9	21.3	20.7	20.7	20.4	21.2	21.9	23.5	24.0	26.5
Norway	10.0	12.0	12.7	14.9	15.2	12.3	14.3	13.9	12.6	12.5
Sweden	15.3	14.1	13.6	12.6	12.7	14.3	15.1	16.0	15.9	20.0
Switzerland	63.4	59.0	58.1	55.8	52.7	49.7	46.3	47.9	49.7	53.0
Outflow data based on residence permits or on other sources:										
Australia										
Permanent departures	18.2	19.2	17.9	20.8	23.4	24.1	24.9	29.9	31.6	33.6
Long-term departures	28.6	30.3	29.4	30.0	42.2	31.9	29.5	29.6	31.8	34.4
Korea	..	..	..	89.1	107.2	114.0	152.3	148.8	266.7	183.0
Mexico	27.0	25.0	21.5	22.6	25.7	26.8	24.4	24.1	30.3	31.7
New Zealand	14.7	16.2	15.9	15.6	28.6	22.4	25.4	29.0	30.6	20.5
United Kingdom	130.6	125.7	151.6	159.6	148.5	173.7	170.6	146.5	173.8	193.7

Source: International Migration Outlook: SOPEMI 2008.

StatLink ᠁᠊᠁ : *http://dx.doi.org/10.1787/430166546443*

Estimating the size of migrant populations ("stocks")

Statisticians face two main issues when it comes to producing international comparisons of the size of immigrant populations in different countries. Firstly, definitions of who is an immigrant vary around the world; and, secondly, countries don't always measure the size of immigrant populations in the same way.

Who is an immigrant?: When it comes to estimating stocks of immigrants, the main focus in some countries – mainly those in Europe as well as Korea and Japan – is on counting "foreign residents". In others, including the traditional settlement countries – Australia, Canada, New Zealand and the United States – the focus is on "foreign born".

This distinction has multiple roots, including differing historical patterns of migration and varying attitudes towards the granting of citizenship and nationality. For instance, in the main settlement countries, immigration has traditionally been seen as part of nation-building: immigrants become American or Australian citizens, and so on. As a result, they no longer stand out as "foreign" in official records, which is why settlement countries focus instead on using "foreign born" as the defining characteristic of immigrant populations. By contrast, in much of Europe, immigrants – and, in some cases, their descendents – have tended to hold on to their own nationality, and indeed often face considerable obstacles if they attempt to switch nationality.

How do countries measure immigrant populations?: Countries rarely specifically set out to measure the numbers of foreign-born people in their populations, but – as with migration flows – there are data sources that can be used to produce estimates, including population registers and residence permits, as well as labour-force surveys and population censuses.

Labour force surveys often include questions about date of birth and nationality and date of arrival, and are thus a useful source of information. But as with any survey, their reliability can be affected by the size of the sample. Also, when it comes to finding out more about the numbers and characteristics of immigrants in the labour force from a particular country, the sample sizes may be so small that they give unreliable results. (See **Table 3**.)

For a more detailed discussion go to *www.oecd.org/els/migration/foreignborn*.

What is the database on immigrants in OECD Countries?

Censuses of various forms have been carried for at least 5 800 years, with the oldest known dating back to Babylon in around 3800 BCE. Carried out every six or seven years, that Babylonian census counted human inhabitants as well as livestock and stocks of commodities like honey and wool. Censuses also existed in ancient China and in the Middle East, and they are mentioned several times in the Bible. In the 18th century, censuses began to be taken in a number of European states, such as Iceland and Sweden, and by the mid-19th century they began taking on formats that are familiar to us today. Typically, this involves a count of the population every ten years, with forms being sent out to households to be completed on a specific day. Today, most, although not all, OECD countries carry out a regular census.

TABLE 3. STOCKS OF FOREIGN-BORN POPULATION IN SELECTED OECD COUNTRIES

Thousands

	1997	1998	1999	2000	2001	2002	2003	2004	2005	2006
Australia	4 314.5	4 332.1	4 369.3	4 412.0	4 482.1	4 565.8	4 655.6	4 736.3	4 840.7	4 956.9
% of total population	23.3	23.2	23.1	23.0	23.1	23.2	23.4	23.6	23.8	24.1
Austria	..	895.7	872.0	843.0	893.9	873.3	923.4	1 059.1	1 100.5	1 151.5
% of total population	..	11.2	10.9	10.5	11.1	10.8	11.4	13.0	13.5	14.1
Belgium	1 011.0	1 023.4	1 042.3	1 058.8	1 112.2	1 151.8	1 185.5	1 220.1	1 268.9	1 319.3
% of total population	9.9	10.0	10.2	10.3	10.8	11.1	11.4	11.7	12.1	12.5
Canada	5 082.5	5 165.6	5 233.8	5 327.0	5 448.5	5 600.7	5 735.9	5 872.3	6 026.9	6 187.0
% of total population	17.7	17.8	18.0	18.1	18.4	18.7	19.0	19.2	19.5	19.8
Czech Republic	..	440.1	455.5	434.0	448.5	471.9	482.2	499.0	523.4	566.3
% of total population	..	4.3	4.4	4.2	4.4	4.6	4.7	4.9	5.1	5.5
Denmark	276.8	287.7	296.9	308.7	321.8	331.5	337.8	343.4	350.4	360.9
% of total population	5.2	5.4	5.6	5.8	6.0	6.2	6.3	6.3	6.5	6.6
Finland	118.1	125.1	131.1	136.2	145.1	152.1	158.9	166.4	176.6	187.9
% of total population	2.3	2.4	2.5	2.6	2.7	2.8	2.9	3.2	3.4	3.6
France	..	..	4 306.0	4 384.6	4 477.9	4 588.3	4 710.6	4 837.6	4 958.5	5 078.3
% of total population	..	..	7.3	7.4	7.5	7.7	7.8	8.0	8.1	8.3
Germany	9 918.7	10 002.3	10 172.7	10 256.1	10 404.9	10 527.7	10 620.8	..	..	..
% of total population	12.1	12.2	12.4	12.5	12.6	12.8	12.9	..	..	..
Greece	..	..	..	..	1 122.9	..	..	..	..	..
% of total population	..	..	..	..	10.3	..	..	..	..	..
Hungary	284.2	286.2	289.3	294.6	300.1	302.8	307.8	319.0	331.5	344.6
% of total population	2.8	2.8	2.9	2.9	3.0	3.0	3.0	3.2	3.3	3.4
Ireland	271.2	288.4	305.9	328.7	356.0	390.0	428.9	468.6	526.6	601.7
% of total population	7.4	7.8	8.2	8.7	9.3	10.0	10.8	11.6	12.7	14.4
Italy	..	..	..	..	1 446.7	..	..	..	..	..
% of total population	..	..	..	..	2.5	..	..	..	..	..
Luxembourg	134.1	137.5	141.9	145.0	144.8	147.0	148.5	150.0	154.0	159.7
% of total population	31.9	32.2	32.8	33.2	32.8	32.9	33.0	33.2	33.8	34.8
Mexico	..	..	..	406.0	..	..	..	..	434.6	..
% of total population	..	..	..	0.5	..	..	..	..	0.4	..
Netherlands	1 469.0	1 513.9	1 556.3	1 615.4	1 674.6	1 714.2	1 731.8	1 736.1	1 734.7	1 732.4
% of total population	9.4	9.6	9.8	10.1	10.4	10.6	10.7	10.6	10.6	10.6
New Zealand	620.8	630.5	643.6	663.0	698.6	737.1	770.5	796.7	840.6	879.5
% of total population	16.4	16.5	16.8	17.2	18.0	18.7	19.2	19.6	20.5	21.2
Norway	257.7	273.2	292.4	305.0	315.2	333.9	347.3	361.1	380.4	405.1
% of total population	5.8	6.1	6.5	6.8	6.9	7.3	7.6	7.8	8.2	8.7
Poland	..	..	..	..	..	776.2	..	..	..	..
% of total population	..	..	..	..	..	1.6	..	..	..	..
Portugal	523.4	516.5	518.8	522.6	651.5	699.1	705.0	714.0	661.0	649.3
% of total population	5.3	5.1	5.1	5.1	6.3	6.7	6.7	6.8	6.3	6.1
Slovak Republic	..	..	..	..	119.1	143.4	171.5	207.6	249.4	301.6
% of total population	..	..	..	..	2.5	2.7	3.2	3.9	4.6	5.6
Spain	1 173.8	1 259.1	1 472.5	1 969.3	2 594.1	3 302.4	3 693.8	4 391.5	4 837.6	5 250.0
% of total population	3.0	3.2	3.7	4.9	6.4	8.0	8.8	10.3	11.1	11.9
Sweden	954.2	968.7	981.6	1 003.8	1 028.0	1 053.5	1 078.1	1 100.3	1 125.8	1 175.2
% of total population	10.8	11.0	11.1	11.3	11.5	11.8	12.0	12.2	12.4	12.9
Switzerland	1 512.8	1 522.8	1 544.8	1 570.8	1 613.8	1 658.7	1 697.8	1 737.7	1 772.8	1 811.2
% of total population	21.3	21.4	21.6	21.9	22.3	22.8	23.1	23.5	23.8	24.1
Turkey	..	..	..	1 278.7	..	..	..	..	..	..
% of total population	..	..	..	1.9	..	..	..	..	..	..
United Kingdom	4 222.4	4 335.1	4 486.9	4 666.9	4 865.6	5 075.6	5 290.2	5 552.7	5 841.8	6 116.4
% of total population	7.2	7.4	7.6	7.9	8.2	8.6	8.9	9.3	9.7	10.1
United States (revised)	29 272.2	29 892.7	29 592.4	31 107.9	32 341.2	35 312.0	36 520.9	37 591.8	38 343.0	39 054.9
% of total population	10.7	10.8	10.6	11.0	11.3	12.3	12.6	12.8	12.9	13.0

See *StatLink* for notes to this table.

Source: International Migration Outlook: SOPEMI 2008.

StatLink 📈 : http://dx.doi.org/10.1787/430220580850

Because census data is comprehensive and typically asks residents to give information on their place of birth, education levels and occupations, it can be a very useful source of information on migrant populations. For this reason, OECD created the Database on Immigrants in OECD Countries, or DIOC, which is based largely on census data, supplemented for some countries or for some categories of information by population registers and labour-force surveys.

That said, there are – inevitably – some limitations. For example, censuses and population registers in different countries don't always ask the same questions or may not ask them in the same ways, so work has to be done to harmonise the information. Also, simply because someone gives their place of birth as "overseas" doesn't make them an immigrant: Some OECD countries have historically had quite high numbers of citizens who were born abroad, such as French citizens who were born in parts of north Africa that were at the time in French possession. And finally, there is an inevitable time lag between the taking of census data, its publication by national authorities, and its processing for inclusion in international databases. Nevertheless, the Database on Immigrants in OECD Countries is a unique and uniquely useful source of information on migrant populations in the OECD area, as the following tables may help to illustrate.

Table 4 shows where existing communities of immigrants in OECD countries come from, as well as the composition of the foreign-born population in terms of age, gender and education levels.

Table 5 offers a more detailed look at the characteristics of immigrants in the OECD area. It shows how many immigrants come from each geographical zone in absolute numbers, as well as their gender mix, educational attainment and employment levels.

Table 6 provides a detailed breakdown of the education levels of native and foreign-born men and women in OECD countries.

TABLE 4. FOREIGN-BORN POPULATION BY COUNTRY OF RESIDENCE
Population figures in thousands

Country of residence	Total population (15+)	Africa	Asia	Latin America	North America	Oceania	EU15	EU10	Other Europe	Un-specified	Total	Of which OECD countries	Population with unknown place of birth (15+)	Proportion of foreign-born in the population (15+) [%]	Women [%]	Tertiary educated [%]	Duration of stay 0-10 years [%]
Australia	14 856.8	166.1	1 043.1	74.3	70.4	407.0	1 667.9	173.4	251.8	6.2	3 860.2	2 242.6	745.2	27.4	50.6	25.8	22.5
Austria	6 679.4	22.4	59.0	9.7	7.6	1.8	185.2	160.4	477.5	-	923.7	461.6	0.8	13.8	52.1	11.3	38.3
Belgium	8 491.5	232.4	62.3	20.0	14.1	1.3	550.9	27.8	110.5	-	1 019.3	674.2	0.5	12.0	51.9	23.0	31.5
Canada	23 900.8	277.5	1 886.9	587.5	246.4	50.0	1 653.6	310.3	342.8	0.3	5 355.2	2 371.9	-	22.4	51.9	38.0	30.0
Switzerland	6 043.4	61.6	93.5	50.1	24.5	4.2	780.7	42.1	308.5	89.0	1 454.2	910.7	250.8	25.1	52.2	23.7	37.6
Czech Republic	8 571.7	1.8	20.7	1.4	2.0	0.3	25.1	310.0	70.7	4.9	437.0	337.6	171.6	5.2	54.5	12.8	24.9
Germany	68 113.6	177.6	965.9	52.8	39.1	-	887.5	1 158.5	3 158.9	1 391.7	7 832.0	3 276.0	5 272.3	12.5	49.7	14.9	20.3
Denmark	4 358.6	26.0	96.5	7.5	9.7	1.9	76.0	16.8	84.9	-	319.3	160.0	23.1	7.4	51.4	23.9	40.8
Spain	34 848.1	372.1	79.3	724.9	19.9	3.7	503.1	23.9	166.3	21.7	1 914.9	616.7	3.2	5.5	49.7	21.1	51.0
Finland	4 244.6	8.1	15.1	1.6	3.6	0.6	35.2	8.8	39.5	-	112.4	45.7	4.5	2.7	50.4	18.9	49.5
France	48 068.4	2 745.3	432.8	85.1	48.5	5.6	1 778.4	132.4	372.0	-	5 600.2	2 222.4	-	11.7	50.5	18.1	17.3
United Kingdom	47 684.5	762.6	1 475.4	324.1	193.3	156.8	1 183.1	202.6	166.1	39.5	4 503.5	1 738.1	-	9.4	53.3	34.8	29.8
Greece	9 273.2	51.0	83.8	6.2	31.0	20.0	130.7	42.3	634.9	-	999.9	282.4	1.1	10.8	49.9	15.9	88.9
Hungary	8 503.4	1.8	10.3	1.0	2.5	0.2	18.5	43.2	198.0	-	275.5	65.1	-	3.2	55.9	19.8	33.8
Ireland	3 034.6	21.5	25.0	2.9	18.0	6.4	236.6	8.8	13.5	0.3	333.0	267.3	-	11.0	50.4	41.1	58.3
Italy	48 892.6	407.5	188.8	219.5	68.0	18.0	459.1	69.8	590.3	-	2 020.9	790.6	-	4.1	54.4	12.2	65.6
Japan	108 224.8	5.1	868.6	193.5	40.0	8.1	17.8	-	3.2	6.1	1 142.4	66.7	15.0	1.1	53.2	30.0	..
Luxembourg	355.3	5.3	3.6	1.4	1.1	0.1	105.8	1.7	9.8	0.9	129.8	110.3	1.6	36.6	50.6	21.7	54.6
Mexico	62 842.6	0.8	9.9	73.1	112.2	0.6	39.4	1.6	3.6	0.3	241.5	157.4	174.3	0.4	49.5	34.8	..
Netherlands	12 733.4	222.8	328.7	297.6	20.6	12.6	278.0	25.5	223.6	10.6	1 419.9	504.4	40.3	11.2	51.4	19.2	28.4
Norway	3 666.9	28.9	93.2	13.8	15.1	1.4	95.3	10.5	44.9	2.8	305.9	139.0	-	8.3	51.1	30.5	44.2
New Zealand	2 889.6	30.0	153.2	4.1	17.9	148.6	252.4	4.8	12.9	0.2	624.1	341.4	119.9	22.5	51.9	31.0	36.5
Poland	31 288.4	2.0	9.6	-	5.8	0.3	132.7	90.8	479.9	15.5	737.7	148.4	516.5	2.4	59.9	11.9	28.4
Portugal	8 699.5	332.4	15.7	66.9	10.4	0.9	134.8	1.1	23.8	-	585.9	151.0	6.7	6.7	50.9	19.3	28.4
Slovak Republic	4 316.4	0.3	1.4	0.2	0.9	-	3.1	92.2	15.0	-	113.2	96.2	405.5	2.9	56.3	15.7	..
Sweden	6 463.9	56.5	224.7	56.1	13.7	3.1	291.6	65.3	222.8	-	933.8	446.0	0.5	14.4	51.4	24.3	32.0
Turkey	47 583.8	4.3	71.9	-	10.8	1.9	361.5	11.8	660.1	8.3	1 130.6	390.7	12.3	2.4	52.2	15.2	..
United States	217 165.2	838.2	7 831.8	16 165.3	868.8	255.6	3 486.8	715.2	1 222.8	5.4	31 389.9	14 732.0	-	14.5	50.4	26.1	36.3
OECD (weighted)	851 796.1	6 862.0	16 150.9	19 041.7	1 915.6	1 111.1	15 370.5	3 751.7	9 908.8	1 603.7	75 715.9	33 746.4	7 758.7	9.0	51.1	24.3	32.8

See *StatLink* for notes to this table.

Source: *A Profile of Immigrant Populations in the 21st Century.*

StatLink : http://dx.doi.org/10.1787/247383367577

TABLE 5. CHARACTERISTICS OF IMMIGRANTS LIVING IN OECD COUNTRIES BY REGION OF ORIGIN

Region of origin	Population 15+ (thousands)			Women (%)	Young (15-24) (%)			Primary educated (%)			Tertiary educated (%)			Employed (%)		
	Men	Women	Total		Men	Women	Total	Men	Women	Total	Men	Women	Total	Men	Women	Total
Africa[1]	3 674	3 188	6 862	46.5	10.8	12.0	11.3	43.2	48.2	45.5	27.0	22.2	24.8	62.9	43.0	53.7
North Africa	1 993	1 643	3 636	45.2	8.2	8.7	8.4	52.9	58.0	55.2	20.0	16.2	18.3	57.0	32.8	46.1
Sub-Saharan Africa	1 509	1 432	2 941	48.7	14.5	15.8	15.1	31.1	36.4	33.7	37.0	29.9	33.6	69.5	54.5	62.2
Asia	7 770	8 381	16 151	51.9	14.8	13.6	14.2	27.0	31.8	29.5	41.0	35.9	38.4	66.2	48.0	56.8
China	981	1 093	2 074	52.7	12.3	11.5	11.9	30.2	34.4	32.4	44.6	38.3	41.3	62.8	47.9	55.0
India	1 021	936	1 957	47.8	10.3	11.1	10.7	22.4	31.1	26.6	57.9	47.8	53.1	74.8	49.3	62.7
Latin America	9 648	9 394	19 042	49.3	19.9	16.0	17.9	56.1	51.5	53.8	12.7	15.2	14.0	65.8	45.6	55.8
Mexico	4 633	3 695	8 329	44.4	23.7	19.6	21.9	70.6	68.3	69.6	5.2	6.4	5.7	66.9	38.7	54.4
North America	875	1 040	1 916	54.3	13.6	11.9	12.7	18.9	20.0	19.5	46.1	41.8	43.8	66.6	47.7	56.4
Oceania	541	570	1 111	51.3	15.8	15.7	15.7	27.3	30.1	28.8	29.0	30.1	29.5	72.8	59.6	66.0
Europe[2]	13 846	15 398	29 245	52.7	10.0	9.2	9.6	39.0	44.4	41.9	23.2	20.8	22.0	60.8	42.4	51.2
EU15	7 254	8 116	15 371	52.8	7.6	7.2	7.4	37.4	42.0	39.8	26.8	23.5	25.0	62.4	44.5	53.0
EU10	1 684	2 068	3 752	55.1	10.0	8.8	9.4	28.1	36.3	32.6	24.2	20.2	22.0	56.6	42.5	48.8
Other Europe	4 805	5 104	9 909	51.5	13.6	12.4	13.0	45.3	51.4	48.4	17.6	16.7	17.2	60.1	39.3	49.4
Unspecified	694	696	1 390	50.1							-	-	-			
Total	37 049	38 667	75 716	51.1	14.1	12.4	13.2	40.9	42.9	41.9	25.1	23.5	24.3	63.4	44.9	53.9
OECD countries	16 524	17 223	33 746	51.0	13.4	11.2	12.3	45.5	45.9	45.7	21.3	20.7	21.0	63.8	43.2	53.3

See StatLink for notes to this table.

Source: A Profile of Immigrant Populations in the 21st Century.

StatLink : http://dx.doi.org/10.1787/247404423511

TABLE 6. EDUCATIONAL ATTAINMENT OF THE NATIVE-BORN AND FOREIGN-BORN POPULATIONS

Percentage of the population aged 15 and above, by country of residence and gender

Country	Education	Native-born			Foreign-born			Total		
		Men [%]	Women [%]	Total [%]	Men [%]	Women [%]	Total [%]	Men [%]	Women [%]	Total [%]
Australia	Primary	41.8	54.9	48.5	34.7	48.0	41.3	40.1	53.2	46.7
	Secondary	40.1	23.4	31.6	39.6	26.1	32.8	39.9	24.1	31.9
	Tertiary	18.1	21.7	20.0	25.6	26.0	25.8	20.0	22.7	21.4
Austria	Primary	24.2	42.0	33.4	45.0	53.4	49.4	27.0	43.5	35.6
	Secondary	61.9	50.0	55.7	41.9	36.9	39.3	59.1	48.2	53.4
	Tertiary	14.0	8.1	10.9	13.2	9.7	11.3	13.9	8.3	11.0
Belgium	Primary	45.3	47.6	46.5	50.5	55.8	53.3	45.9	48.5	47.3
	Secondary	31.5	28.9	30.1	24.4	23.1	23.8	30.7	28.2	29.4
	Tertiary	23.2	23.5	23.3	25.1	21.0	23.0	23.4	23.2	23.3
Canada	Primary	32.6	30.7	31.6	27.6	32.4	30.1	31.5	31.1	31.3
	Secondary	39.1	34.8	36.9	33.4	30.6	31.9	37.9	33.8	35.8
	Tertiary	28.2	34.5	31.5	39.0	37.0	38.0	30.6	35.1	32.9
Switzerland	Primary	18.6	32.4	25.6	38.0	44.9	41.6	23.0	35.6	29.5
	Secondary	54.9	57.6	56.3	34.1	35.2	34.7	50.4	52.2	51.3
	Tertiary	26.5	9.9	18.1	27.9	19.9	23.7	26.6	12.1	19.2
Czech Rep.	Primary	16.5	28.7	22.8	27.4	47.9	38.6	17.2	29.9	23.8
	Secondary	71.5	62.8	67.0	56.5	42.1	48.7	70.7	61.5	65.9
	Tertiary	12.0	8.5	10.2	16.1	9.9	12.8	12.2	8.5	10.3
Germany	Primary	16.8	31.0	24.2	41.2	50.5	45.8	20.4	33.7	27.2
	Secondary	58.0	55.1	56.5	42.1	36.4	39.3	55.7	52.6	54.1
	Tertiary	25.1	13.8	19.3	16.7	13.1	14.9	24.0	13.7	18.7
Denmark	Primary	35.0	40.1	37.6	35.2	38.6	36.9	35.0	40.0	37.5
	Secondary	46.2	39.0	42.6	39.9	38.5	39.2	45.8	39.0	42.3
	Tertiary	18.8	20.9	19.9	25.0	22.9	23.9	19.2	21.0	20.1
Spain	Primary	65.3	67.5	66.4	58.1	54.6	56.3	64.9	66.8	65.9
	Secondary	16.3	14.9	15.6	21.4	23.7	22.6	16.6	15.4	15.9
	Tertiary	18.4	17.6	18.0	20.5	21.7	21.1	18.6	17.8	18.2
Finland	Primary	39.7	40.8	40.3	53.1	52.1	52.6	40.1	41.1	40.6
	Secondary	38.4	34.3	36.3	30.0	27.0	28.5	38.2	34.1	36.1
	Tertiary	21.9	24.9	23.4	16.9	20.9	18.9	21.7	24.8	23.3
France	Primary	41.5	49.6	45.8	52.0	57.5	54.8	42.8	50.5	46.8
	Secondary	41.6	33.5	37.4	28.9	25.5	27.2	40.1	32.6	36.2
	Tertiary	16.8	16.9	16.9	19.1	17.0	18.1	17.1	16.9	17.0
United Kingdom	Primary	50.9	51.5	51.2	39.8	41.3	40.6	49.9	50.5	50.2
	Secondary	28.1	29.2	28.7	23.9	25.1	24.5	27.7	28.8	28.3
	Tertiary	20.9	19.3	20.1	36.3	33.6	34.8	22.4	20.8	21.6
Greece	Primary	50.2	54.7	52.5	46.6	38.8	42.7	49.8	52.9	51.4
	Secondary	34.2	32.9	33.5	39.6	43.3	41.4	34.8	34.0	34.4
	Tertiary	15.5	12.5	14.0	13.8	17.9	15.9	15.4	13.1	14.2
Hungary	Primary	39.5	50.1	45.1	35.6	45.4	41.1	39.4	49.9	45.0
	Secondary	49.2	39.7	44.2	40.7	37.8	39.1	49.0	39.7	44.0
	Tertiary	11.3	10.2	10.7	23.6	16.7	19.8	11.6	10.4	11.0
Ireland	Primary	50.0	45.6	47.8	29.9	29.4	29.6	47.8	43.8	45.8
	Secondary	28.6	30.3	29.5	29.2	29.4	29.3	28.7	30.2	29.5
	Tertiary	21.4	24.1	22.7	40.9	41.2	41.1	23.5	25.9	24.7
Italy	Primary	62.4	64.8	63.6	56.6	52.3	54.3	62.2	64.3	63.3
	Secondary	29.3	27.3	28.3	32.0	34.8	33.5	29.4	27.6	28.5
	Tertiary	8.3	7.9	8.1	11.4	12.9	12.2	8.4	8.1	8.3

Country	Education	Native-born Men [%]	Native-born Women [%]	Native-born Total [%]	Foreign-born Men [%]	Foreign-born Women [%]	Foreign-born Total [%]	Total Men [%]	Total Women [%]	Total Total [%]
Japan	Primary	23.4	26.6	25.1	23.7	27.7	25.9	23.4	26.6	25.1
	Secondary	45.9	48.3	47.1	42.7	45.4	44.2	45.9	48.3	47.1
	Tertiary	30.7	25.1	27.8	33.6	26.8	30.0	30.7	25.2	27.8
Luxembourg	Primary	23.3	33.9	28.7	34.5	38.9	36.7	27.4	35.8	31.7
	Secondary	61.5	55.7	58.6	42.2	41.0	41.6	54.5	50.3	52.4
	Tertiary	15.2	10.4	12.8	23.3	20.1	21.7	18.1	13.9	16.0
Mexico	Primary	69.5	71.4	70.5	37.4	40.6	39.0	69.4	71.3	70.4
	Secondary	16.3	17.1	16.7	24.0	28.5	26.2	16.3	17.1	16.7
	Tertiary	14.2	11.5	12.8	38.6	30.9	34.8	14.3	11.6	12.8
Netherlands	Primary	35.1	45.8	40.5	47.9	50.4	49.2	36.5	46.3	41.5
	Secondary	43.3	38.1	40.6	30.8	32.4	31.6	41.9	37.4	39.6
	Tertiary	21.6	16.1	18.8	21.3	17.2	19.2	21.6	16.2	18.9
Norway	Primary	18.2	22.4	20.3	17.3	19.3	18.3	18.2	22.2	20.2
	Secondary	59.4	54.1	56.7	53.8	48.7	51.2	59.0	53.7	56.3
	Tertiary	22.4	23.6	23.0	28.9	32.0	30.5	22.8	24.1	23.5
New Zealand	Primary	30.9	29.4	30.1	18.4	18.9	18.7	28.2	27.1	27.6
	Secondary	40.2	45.0	42.7	48.7	51.9	50.4	42.1	46.6	44.4
	Tertiary	28.9	25.6	27.2	32.8	29.2	31.0	29.7	26.3	27.9
Poland	Primary	28.7	33.6	31.2	38.5	54.1	47.9	28.9	34.1	31.6
	Secondary	61.6	55.4	58.4	45.8	36.6	40.3	61.3	54.9	57.9
	Tertiary	9.8	11.0	10.4	15.7	9.3	11.9	9.9	11.0	10.5
Portugal	Primary	80.9	79.3	80.0	57.3	52.3	54.7	79.2	77.5	78.3
	Secondary	12.2	12.2	12.2	25.5	26.3	25.9	13.2	13.1	13.1
	Tertiary	6.9	8.5	7.7	17.2	21.4	19.3	7.6	9.4	8.5
Slovak Republic	Primary	22.0	33.4	28.0	20.2	36.4	29.3	22.2	33.9	28.3
	Secondary	66.1	57.1	61.4	59.1	51.9	55.0	66.0	56.8	61.2
	Tertiary	11.9	9.5	10.6	20.7	11.7	15.7	11.8	9.3	10.5
Sweden	Primary	26.8	23.1	25.0	28.8	30.2	29.5	27.1	24.1	25.6
	Secondary	53.8	50.5	52.2	48.1	44.4	46.2	53.1	49.7	51.4
	Tertiary	19.3	26.3	22.8	23.0	25.4	24.3	19.8	26.2	23.0
Turkey	Primary	70.2	81.2	75.6	49.9	57.1	53.6	69.7	80.6	75.1
	Secondary	21.2	13.8	17.6	33.7	28.8	31.2	21.5	14.2	17.9
	Tertiary	8.6	5.0	6.8	16.4	14.1	15.2	8.8	5.3	7.0
United States	Primary	21.2	19.6	20.3	40.3	38.1	39.2	24.0	22.2	23.1
	Secondary	50.9	53.4	52.2	33.1	36.2	34.7	48.2	51.0	49.7
	Tertiary	28.0	27.0	27.4	26.6	25.6	26.1	27.8	26.8	27.3
OECD (weighted)	Primary	38.1	41.5	39.9	40.9	42.9	41.9	38.3	41.6	40.0
	Secondary	40.9	39.6	40.2	34.0	33.6	33.8	40.3	39.2	39.7
	Tertiary	21.0	18.8	19.9	25.1	23.5	24.3	21.4	19.2	20.3
OECD (unweighted)	Primary	38.6	44.0	41.4	38.8	43.1	41.1	39.0	44.2	41.7
	Secondary	42.9	39.1	40.9	37.3	35.3	36.2	42.1	38.4	40.2
	Tertiary	18.5	16.9	17.7	23.9	21.6	22.7	19.0	17.4	18.2

See *StatLink* for notes to this table.

Source: *A Profile of Immigrant Populations in the 21st Century.*

StatLink 🖳 : http://dx.doi.org/10.1787/247577762467

TABLE 7. OCCUPATIONS OF THE NATIVE-BORN AND FOREIGN-BORN

Percentage of the population aged 15 and above, by country of residence and gender

Country	Education	Native-born			Foreign-born			Total		
		Men (%)	Women (%)	Total (%)	Men (%)	Women (%)	Total (%)	Men (%)	Women (%)	Total (%)
Australia	Professionals	29.6	29.1	29.4	32.2	29.9	31.2	30.3	29.2	29.8
	Technicians	15.7	38.6	26.3	15.5	35.5	24.2	15.7	37.9	25.7
	Operators	54.7	32.3	44.4	52.3	34.7	44.7	54.1	32.9	44.5
Austria	Professionals	20.1	14.1	17.4	15.0	10.9	13.3	19.3	13.7	16.8
	Technicians	27.2	44.0	34.8	14.7	26.1	19.7	25.5	41.6	32.7
	Operators	52.7	41.9	47.8	70.3	62.9	67.1	55.2	44.7	50.5
Belgium	Professionals	28.5	32.7	30.3	30.1	34.1	31.6	28.6	32.8	30.4
	Technicians	23.9	33.1	27.8	18.5	27.7	22.0	23.3	32.6	27.3
	Operators	47.7	34.2	41.9	51.4	38.2	46.4	48.1	34.6	42.3
Canada	Professionals	25.3	25.3	25.3	32.1	25.1	28.8	26.7	25.3	26.0
	Technicians	17.2	41.8	28.8	17.0	36.6	26.0	17.1	40.7	28.2
	Operators	57.6	32.9	45.9	51.0	38.3	45.2	56.2	34.0	45.8
Switzerland	Professionals	31.4	16.2	25.1	26.8	18.0	23.1	30.4	16.6	24.6
	Technicians	26.4	52.8	37.4	20.1	36.9	27.2	25.0	49.3	35.2
	Operators	42.2	31.0	37.6	53.1	45.2	49.8	44.6	34.1	40.2
Czech Rep.	Professionals	16.4	16.3	16.4	19.7	17.2	18.6	16.6	16.3	16.4
	Technicians	21.0	39.6	29.5	17.0	26.9	21.4	20.9	39.1	29.1
	Operators	62.5	44.1	54.2	63.2	55.9	60.0	62.6	44.6	54.4
Germany	Professionals	23.2	14.9	19.5	11.5	8.4	10.2	21.7	14.2	18.4
	Technicians	24.1	48.6	35.1	13.7	29.3	20.5	22.8	46.4	33.4
	Operators	52.7	36.5	45.5	74.8	62.2	69.3	55.4	39.5	48.3
Denmark	Professionals	20.5	15.6	18.1	18.7	14.8	16.9	20.4	15.5	18.0
	Technicians	20.9	44.1	32.2	16.9	30.6	23.3	20.7	43.4	31.7
	Operators	58.6	40.3	49.7	64.5	54.6	59.8	58.9	41.1	50.2
Spain	Professionals	18.0	22.2	19.6	15.2	15.9	15.5	17.8	21.7	19.3
	Technicians	16.2	26.3	20.0	10.9	18.7	14.0	15.9	25.8	19.6
	Operators	65.8	51.5	60.5	73.9	65.4	70.5	66.3	52.5	61.1
Finland	Professionals	19.5	18.2	18.8	23.0	19.8	21.6	19.6	18.2	18.9
	Technicians	20.8	33.7	27.1	17.9	23.3	20.2	20.8	33.5	27.0
	Operators	59.7	48.1	54.0	59.1	56.9	58.1	59.7	48.2	54.1
France	Professionals	21.0	14.7	18.1	23.5	18.5	22.1	21.3	14.9	18.4
	Technicians	22.9	45.6	33.3	16.3	37.3	22.4	22.1	45.1	32.3
	Operators	56.2	39.8	48.6	60.2	44.2	55.5	56.6	40.0	49.3
United Kingdom	Professionals	30.2	21.8	26.3	39.4	28.2	34.2	31.0	22.3	27.0
	Technicians	17.1	38.2	26.8	17.0	36.5	26.0	17.1	38.0	26.8
	Operators	52.7	40.0	46.9	43.6	35.3	39.8	51.9	39.6	46.3
Greece	Professionals	22.6	25.2	23.5	9.3	14.6	11.2	20.7	23.8	21.8
	Technicians	14.0	29.2	19.6	5.9	14.5	9.0	12.9	27.3	18.2
	Operators	63.4	45.6	56.8	84.8	70.9	79.9	66.4	49.0	60.0
Hungary	Professionals	19.3	22.1	20.6	33.6	29.7	31.8	19.7	22.4	20.9
	Technicians	12.1	34.8	22.6	12.6	28.8	20.1	12.1	34.6	22.5
	Operators	68.6	43.1	56.8	53.8	41.4	48.1	68.2	43.1	56.6

Country	Education	Native-born			Foreign-born			Total		
		Men (%)	Women (%)	Total (%)	Men (%)	Women (%)	Total (%)	Men (%)	Women (%)	Total (%)
Ireland	Professionals	27.3	34.5	30.3	37.6	38.8	38.1	28.5	35.0	31.2
	Technicians	12.0	31.5	20.1	12.8	29.4	19.9	12.1	31.3	20.1
	Operators	60.7	34.0	49.7	49.6	31.8	42.0	59.4	33.7	48.7
Italy	Professionals	23.1	18.1	21.1	18.8	15.6	17.5	22.9	18.0	21.0
	Technicians	19.4	37.1	26.3	14.3	28.5	19.9	19.1	36.6	26.0
	Operators	57.5	44.8	52.5	66.9	55.9	62.6	58.0	45.4	53.0
Luxembourg	Professionals	21.4	18.9	20.4	25.4	20.2	23.3	23.1	19.5	21.6
	Technicians	36.7	54.1	43.7	21.0	30.3	24.8	30.1	43.8	35.7
	Operators	41.9	27.0	35.8	53.6	49.5	51.9	46.8	36.7	42.7
Mexico	Professionals	8.2	11.6	9.2	37.1	33.8	36.1	8.3	11.7	9.3
	Technicians	9.0	22.0	13.1	13.3	27.9	17.7	9.0	22.0	13.1
	Operators	82.9	66.4	77.7	49.6	38.4	46.2	82.7	66.3	77.6
Netherlands	Professionals	35.2	24.9	30.8	27.9	21.8	25.3	34.5	24.6	30.3
	Technicians	22.5	41.3	30.6	19.5	38.4	27.6	22.2	41.0	30.3
	Operators	42.3	33.8	38.6	52.5	39.8	47.1	43.3	34.3	39.4
Norway	Professionals	24.3	13.9	19.4	23.0	18.5	20.9	24.3	14.2	19.5
	Technicians	24.3	38.9	31.2	21.9	30.7	26.0	24.2	38.5	30.9
	Operators	51.4	47.1	49.4	55.2	50.8	53.1	51.6	47.3	49.6
New Zealand	Professionals	25.7	27.8	26.7	34.3	32.5	33.4	27.3	28.7	28.0
	Technicians	15.6	35.5	24.9	18.3	33.3	25.3	16.1	35.1	25.0
	Operators	58.8	36.7	48.4	47.4	34.2	41.3	56.6	36.2	47.1
Poland	Professionals	17.0	22.2	19.5	32.3	33.2	32.7	17.2	22.3	19.6
	Technicians	13.3	29.6	20.9	13.8	22.9	17.6	13.3	29.5	20.8
	Operators	69.7	48.2	59.7	53.9	43.9	49.7	69.5	48.1	59.6
Portugal	Professionals	14.9	15.2	15.1	19.9	23.1	21.3	15.4	15.9	15.6
	Technicians	16.6	24.9	20.3	19.5	31.1	24.8	16.9	25.4	20.7
	Operators	68.4	59.9	64.6	60.7	45.8	53.9	67.8	58.6	63.7
Slovak Republic	Professionals	17.4	21.3	19.2	25.3	22.3	23.8	17.5	21.4	19.3
	Technicians	19.2	36.9	27.4	19.6	33.1	26.1	19.2	36.8	27.3
	Operators	63.5	41.8	53.4	55.1	44.6	50.0	63.3	41.8	53.3
Sweden	Professionals	25.8	22.8	24.3	20.2	17.9	19.0	25.2	22.3	23.8
	Technicians	24.5	34.7	29.5	17.9	24.4	21.2	23.8	33.6	28.6
	Operators	49.7	42.5	46.2	61.9	57.7	59.8	50.9	44.2	47.6
OECD (weighted)	Professionals	20.9	19.0	20.1	24.3	20.4	22.6	21.2	19.1	20.3
	Technicians	17.8	37.4	26.1	15.5	32.1	22.5	17.6	37.0	25.9
	Operators	61.4	43.6	53.8	60.2	47.5	54.9	61.2	43.9	53.8
OECD (unweighted)	Professionals	22.6	20.8	21.8	25.3	22.5	24.1	22.7	20.8	21.8
	Technicians	19.7	37.5	27.6	16.2	29.5	21.9	19.1	36.4	26.7
	Operators	57.7	41.7	50.7	58.5	47.9	54.1	58.2	42.8	51.4

See *StatLink* for notes to this table.

Source: A Profile of Immigrant Populations in the 21st Century.

StatLink ▓▒▓▒ : *http://dx.doi.org/10.1787/248322247831*

Table 7 provides an opportunity to compare the jobs that locals do with those undertaken by immigrants. The three categories it uses are based on the International Standard Classification of Occupations (ISCO),* and broadly correspond to the following types of work:

Professionals (ISCO groups 1 and 2): Corporate, departmental and general managers; professionals, such as architects, engineers, teachers and medical professionals (except nurses).

Technicians (ISCO groups 3 and 4): Associate professionals, nurses, business service agents and clerks.

Operators (and labourers) (ISCO groups 5-9): Shop workers, fisheries and agriculture workers, craft and trades workers, machine operators, labourers cleaners.

Broadly speaking, the proportions of native-born workers in each of these categories don't vary all that much between different OECD countries – generally, about 30% of workers are in the technician camp and 40-60% in the labourer group. There's much greater differentiation among immigrants. For example, in Germany only about 10% of immigrants are working in the professional category with around 70% in the operators and labourers category; by contrast, in the United Kingdom, more than a third, or 34%, are in the professionals group with just under 40% in the operators category. New Zealand, which has a highly selective immigration policy, has figures that are broadly similar to the UK's.

* For the full ISCO listing, go to *http://laborsta.ilo.org/applv8/data/isco88e.html*.

Find Out More

FROM OECD...

On the Internet
For OECD statistics on international migration, go to *www.sourceoecd.org/database/oecdstat*, and click on "OECD.stat"; then click on "Demography and Population" and then "Migration Statistics". Two databases are available: **International Migration Database,** which contains OECD's most up-to-date data on international migration; and **Database on Immigrants in OECD Countries,** which is based largely on data from the 20 000 round of censuses in OECD countries. OECD data can be also accessed *via www.oecd.org/statistics,* and from there by clicking on the "Demography and Population" link. (*Note:* Access to OECD databases may be available to some users for trial periods only.)

Publications
International Migration Outlook: SOPEMI: Published annually, the Outlook provides the latest data on migration movements in the OECD area as well as assessments of the size of foreign and foreign-born populations and numbers of naturalisations. There are also notes on individual OECD member countries detailing recent developments in their migration movements and polices. Each edition also includes special chapters devoted to topical issues in migration.
A Profile of Immigrant Populations in the 21st Century: Data from OECD Countries (2008): Based on the most recent round of censuses in OECD countries, this book presents a comprehensive picture of the origin and structural characteristics of immigrant populations in OECD countries. There are nine thematic chapters covering issues including the age structures of immigrant populations, education and employment levels and migrants' occupations. Other issues covered include the gender dimension of the brain drain and the migration of health professionals.

Also of interest:
Standardised Statistics on Immigrant Inflows (2007): This paper from OECD's Directorate for Employment, Labour and Social Affairs discusses some of the OECD's work on standardising data on immigration. Available at *www.oecd.org/dataoecd/39/29/38832099.pdf.*

The Comparability of International Migration Statistics (2005): This OECD Statistics Brief discusses some of the main challenges in producing internationally comparable migration statistics. Available at *www.oecd.org/dataoecd/4/41/35082073.pdf.*

... AND OTHER SOURCES

International Data Base (*www.census.gov/ipc/www/idb*): Maintained by the US Census Bureau, this database carries information from censuses carried out in more than 200 countries and areas of the world.

MPI Immigration Data Hub (*www.migrationinformation.org/datahub*): The Migration Policy Institute, a US-based independent think tank on migration issues, maintains a database on international migration.

The Estimation of Illegal Migration in Europe (2004): This paper by Michael Jandl of the International Centre for Migration Policy Development looks at some of the issues involved in calculating the scale of irregular migration in Europe. Available at *www.net4you.com/jandlftp/Estimation-2004.pdf.*

Recommendations on Statistics of International Migration (1998): The latest revision of the UN's recommendations for the compilation of statistics on international migration. Available at *http://unstats.un.org/unsd/publication/SeriesM/SeriesM_58rev1E.pdf.*

References

Chapter 1

Ban, K.M. (2007), "We Should Welcome the Dawn of the Migration Age", 10 July, *The Guardian*, Guardian News and Media Ltd., Manchester, UK.

Economist, The (2009), "The People Crunch", 17 January, *The Economist*, The Economist Newspapers Ltd., London.

Gurría, A. (2007), Speech at the presentation of *Gaining from Migration* to the High Level Conference on Legal Immigration, 13 September, Lisbon, Portugal, accessed at *www.oecd.org*.

Hitt, G. (2007), "Poll Finds Americans Turning Inward Before Vote", 21 December, *The Wall Street Journal*, News Corp., New York.

Lahav, G. and A.M. Messina (eds) (2006), *The Migration Reader: Exploring Politics and Policies*, Lynne Rienner Publishers, Inc. Boulder, CO.

Martin, J.P. (2008), "Migration and the Global Economy: Some Stylised Facts", a paper from the Directorate for Employment, Labour and Social Affairs, OECD, Paris; accessed at *www.oecd.org/dataoecd/27/54/40196342.pdf*.

OECD (2007), *International Migration Outlook: SOPEMI 2007*, OECD Publishing, Paris.

OECD (2008), *International Migration Outlook: SOPEMI 2008*, OECD Publishing, Paris.

OECD (2008), *OECD Annual Report 2008*, OECD Publishing, Paris, *www.oecd.org/dataoecd/39/19/40556222.pdf*.

OECD (2008), *OECD Factbook 2008: Economic, Environmental and Social Statistics*, OECD Publishing, Paris.

Papademetriou, D.G and A. Terrazas (2009), "Immigrants and the Current Economic Crisis: Research Evidence", *Policy Challenges and Implications*, Migration Policy Institute, Washington DC.

Parker, G. (2007), "No Immigration Please, We're British and Unconvinced", *Financial Times*, Financial Times Ltd., London.

OECD Insights: International Migration

Chapter 2

Alagiah, G. (2004), "Migration: 'A Force of History'", British Broadcasting Co., London, last updated on 18 May, *http://news.bbc.co.uk/2/hi/3523208.stm.*

Barton, H.A. (1975), *Letters from the Promised Land: Swedes in America, 1840-1914,* University of Minnesota Press, Minneapolis.

Bohlen, C. (2007) "Letter from Russia: A Boom that Depends on Migrant Workers", 23 October, *The International Herald Tribune,* The New York Times Co., New York.

Castles, S. and M.J. Miller (2003), *The Age of Migration: International Population Movements in the Modern World* (3rd ed.), Palgrave Macmillan, Houndmills, UK.

Chanda, N. (2007), *Bound Together: How Traders, Preachers, Warriors and Adventurers Shaped Globalisation,* Yale University Press, New Haven, CT.

Cohen, R. (1995), "European Colonisation and Settlement", *in* Cohen, R. (ed.), *The Cambridge Survey of World Migration,* Cambridge University Press, Cambridge.

Elder, C. (2003), "Invaders, Illegals and Aliens: Imagining Exclusion in a 'White Australia'", Vol. 7, *Law/Text/Culture,* University of Wollongong, NSW, Australia.

Hatton, T.J. and J.G. Williamson (1998), *The Age of Mass Migration: Causes and Economic Impact,* Oxford University Press, Oxford.

Lowell, B.L. (2007) "Trends in International Migration Flows and Stocks, 1975-2005", *OECD Social, Employment And Migration Working Paper,* No. 58, OECD Publishing, Paris.

Martin, J.P. (2008), "Migration and the Global Economy: Some Stylised Facts", a paper from Directorate for Employment, Labour and Social Affairs, OECD Publishing, Paris, *www.oecd.org/dataoecd/27/54/40196342.pdf.*

New York Times, The (1892), "Landed On Ellis Island", 2 January, *The New York Times,* New York.

Nickerson, C. (2006) "A Lesson in Immigration", 19 April, *The Boston Globe,* The New York Times Co., New York.

Noirel, G. (1995), "Italians and Poles in France, 1880-1945", *in* Cohen, R. (ed.), *The Cambridge Survey of World Migration,* Cambridge University Press, Cambridge.

OECD (2004), *Trade and Migration: Building Bridges for Global Labour Mobility,* OECD Publishing, Paris.

OECD (2006), *International Migration Outlook: SOPEMI 2006,* OECD Publishing, Paris.

OECD (2006), *Where Immigrant Students Succeed: A Comparative Review of Performance and Engagement in PISA 2003,* OECD Publishing, Paris.

OECD (2007), *International Migration Outlook: SOPEMI 2007,* OECD Publishing, Paris.

OECD (2008), *International Migration Outlook: SOPEMI 2008,* OECD Publishing, Paris.

Ogden, P.E. (1995), "Labour Migration to France", in Cohen, R. (ed.), *The Cambridge Survey of World Migration,* Cambridge University Press, Cambridge.

Stix, G. (2008) "The Migration History of Humans: DNA Study Traces Human Origins Across the Continents", 7 July, *Scientific American Magazine,* Scientific American Inc., New York.

Tinker, H. (1995), "The British Colonies of Settlement", *in* Cohen, R. (ed.), *The Cambridge Survey of World Migration,* Cambridge University Press, Cambridge.

Zimmermann, K.F. (1995), "Tackling the European Migration Problem", Spring, Vol. 9, No. 2, *The Journal of Economic Perspectives,* American Economic Association, Pittsburgh, PA.

Chapter 3

Anderson, S. and M. Platzer (2006), *American Made: The Impact of Immigrant Entrepreneurs and Professionals on US Competitiveness,* National Venture Capital Association, *www.nvca.org/pdf/AmericanMade_study.pdf.*

BBC News (2004), "Attacking Europe's border fences", *www.bbcnews.com,* last updated 30 March.

BBC News (2004), "Billy's Journey: Europe at Last", *www.bbcnews.com,* last updated 30 March.

Dayton-Johnson, J., L.T. Katseli *et al.* (2007), *Gaining from Migration: Towards a New Mobility System,* OECD Publishing, Paris.

Downes, L. (2007), "The Word that Paralyses Debate", *International Herald Tribune,* 30 October, New York Times Co., New York.

Georges Tapinos, G. (2000), "Illegal Immigrants and the Labour Market", February, *OECD Observer,* OECD, Paris.

International Organisation for Migration (2003), "Ways to Curb the Growing Complexities of Irregular Migration", *World Migration 2003,* International Organisation for Migration, Geneva.

Lowell, B.L. (2007), "Trends in International Migration Flows and Stocks, 1975-2005", *OECD Social, Employment and Migration Working Papers,* No. 58, OECD Publishing, Paris.

Maley, P. (2009), "Employers Keep Faith in their Migrant Workers", 20 March, The Australian News Ltd., Sydney, NSW.

Mclean, R. (2005), "5 African Migrants Killed and Scores Hurt at Spanish Enclave Fence", 30 September, *International Herald Tribune,* The New York Times Co., New York.

Migrant Rights Centre Ireland (2007), *Life in the Shadows: An Exploration of Irregular Migration in Ireland,* Migrant Rights Centre Ireland, Dublin.

Miller, M.J. (1995), "Illegal Migration", *in* Cohen, R. (ed.), *The Cambridge Survey of World Migration,* Cambridge University Press, Cambridge.

O'Brien, B. (2007), "Forced Labour of Migrants Amounts to Slavery", 30 June, *The Irish Times,* Dublin.

OECD (2003), "Service Providers on the Move", *OECD Policy Briefs,* August, OECD Publishing, Paris.

OECD (2004), *International Migration Outlook SOPEMI 2004,* OECD Publishing, Paris.

OECD (2004), *Migration for Employment: Bilateral Agreements at a Crossroads,* OECD Publishing, Paris.

OECD (2004), *Trade and Migration: Building Bridges for Global Labour Mobility,* OECD Publishing, Paris.

OECD (2006), *International Migration Outlook SOPEMI 2006,* OECD Publishing, Paris.

OECD (2007), *International Migration Outlook SOPEMI 2007,* OECD Publishing, Paris.

OECD (2007), *Policy Coherence for Development: Migration and Developing Countries,* OECD Publishing, Paris.

OECD (2008), *International Migration Outlook: SOPEMI 2008,* OECD Publishing, Paris.

OECD (2008), *OECD Factbook: Economic, Environmental and Social Statistics,* OECD Publishing, Paris.

OECD (2009), *International Migration Outlook: SOPEMI 2009,* OECD Publishing, Paris.

Pew Global Attitudes Project, The (2007), "World Publics Welcome Global Trade – But Not Immigration", 4 October, Pew Research Centre, Washington DC, *www.pewglobal.org/reports/pdf/258.pdf.*

Roberts, A. (2008), "Keep Out", 5-11 January, *The Economist,* The Economist Newspaper Ltd., London.

Sciolino, E. (2007), "Immigration, Black Sheep and Swiss Rage", 8 October, *The New York Times,* New York.

Wadhwa, V. *et al.* (2007), America's New Immigrant Entrepreneurs, 4 January, Duke University/UC Berkeley, *http://memp.pratt.duke.edu/downloads/americas_new_immigrant_entrepreneurs.pdf.*

Chapter 4

Bosch, X. (2003), "Brain Drain Robbing Europe of its Brightest Young Scientists", Vol. 361, Issue No. 9376, 28 June, *The Lancet,* Elsevier Ltd., London.

Field, S., M. Kuczera and B. Pont (2007), *No More Failures: Ten Steps to Equity in Education,* OECD Publishing, Paris.

Garcia, E.E. and B. Jensen (2006), *Dual-Language Programs in US Schools: An Alternative to Monocultural, Monolingual Education,* National Institute for Early Education Research, Rutgers University, N.J., *http://nieer.org/docs/?DocID=167.*

Jean, S., O. Causa *et al.* (2007), "Migration in OECD Countries: Labour Market Impact and Integration Issues", *OECD Economics Department Working Papers,* No. 562, OECD Publishing, Paris.

Lewin, T. (2007), "Foreign Students Contribute a Lot to US Economy", 12 November, *International Herald Tribune,* New York Times Co., New York.

Lowell, B.L. (2007), "Trends in International Migration Flows and Stocks, 1975-2005", *OECD Social, Employment and Migration Working Papers,* No. 58, OECD Publishing, Paris.

Mac Cormaic, R. (2007), "Room at the Inn as Festive Cheer Fills the School No One Expected", 11 December, *The Irish Times,* Dublin.

OECD (1999), *Trends in International Migration SOPEMI 1999,* OECD Publishing, Paris.

OECD (2001), *Trends in International Migration SOPEMI 2001,* OECD Publishing, Paris.

OECD (2004), *Internationalisation and Trade in Higher Education: Opportunities and Challenges,* OECD Publishing, Paris.

OECD (2006), *Starting Strong II: Early Childhood Education and Care,* OECD Publishing, Paris.

OECD (2006), *Where Immigrant Students Succeed: A Comparative Review of Performance and Engagement in PISA 2003,* OECD Publishing, Paris.

OECD (2007), *Education at a Glance 2007: OECD Indicators,* OECD Publishing, Paris.

OECD (2007), *PISA 2006: Science Competencies for Tomorrow's World,* Vol. 1: Analysis, OECD Publishing, Paris.

OECD (2008), *Education at a Glance 2008: OECD Indicators,* OECD Publishing, Paris.

Sullivan, K. (2007), "Hustling to Find Classrooms for all in a Diverse Ireland", 24 October, *The Washington Post,* Washington DC.

Tremblay, K. (2001), "Student Mobility between and towards OECD Countries: A Comparative Analysis", *International Mobility of the Highly Skilled,* OECD Publishing, Paris.

Chapter 5

Benseman, J. and J. Comings (2008), "Case Study: United States", in *Teaching, Learning and Assessment for Adults: Improving Foundation Skills,* OECD Publishing, Paris.

Block, I. (2007), "From Aerospace Engineering to Plastic Toys: Diploma Holder's Plight Highlights Problems Immigrants Face", 11 September, *The Gazette* (Montreal), CanWest Publishing Inc., Montreal.

Borjas, G.J. (2007), "'Do No Evil'", 25 June, *National Review Online,* National Review Inc., New York.

Bracken, A. (2008), "Arrivals: Dr. Jean-Pierre Eyanga, 53, The Congo", 9 March, *Sunday Tribune,* Tribune Newspapers PLC, Dublin.

Card, D. (2005), "Is the New Immigration Really So Bad?", August, Working Paper 11547, National Bureau of Economic Research, Cambridge, MA.

Davis, B. (1996), "Despite his Heritage, Prominent Economist Backs Immigration Cut", 26 April, *The Wall Street Journal,* Dow Jones and Co., New York.

Field, S., M. Kuczera and B. Pont (2007), *No More Failures: Ten Steps to Equity in Education,* OECD Publishing, Paris.

House of Lords Select Committee on Economic Affairs (2008), *The Economic Impact of Immigration,* Vol. 1: Report, The Stationery Office, London.

Jean, S. *et al.* (2007), "Migration in OECD Countries: Labour Market Impact and Integration Issues", *OECD Economics Department Working Paper,* No. 562, OECD Publishing, Paris, *http://dx.doi.org/10.1787/164604735126*

Jean, S. and M. Jimenez (2007), "The Unemployment Impact of Immigration in OECD Countries", *OECD Economics Department Working Papers,* No. 563, OECD, Paris.

Keeley, B. (2007), *Human Capital: How What You Know Shapes Your Life,* OECD Publishing, Paris.

Looney, J. (2008), *Teaching, Learning and Assessment for Adults: Improving Foundation Skills,* OECD Publishing, Paris.

OECD (2004), *Trade and Migration: Building Bridges for Global Labour Mobility,* OECD Publishing, Paris.

OECD (2005), *OECD Economic Surveys: Greece,* OECD Publishing, Paris.

OECD (2006), *From Immigration to Integration: Local Solutions to a Global Challenge,* OECD Publishing, Paris.

OECD (2006), *International Migration Outlook: SOPEMI 2006,* OECD Publishing, Paris.

OECD (2007), *International Migration Outlook: SOPEMI 2007,* OECD Publishing, Paris.

OECD (2007), *Jobs for Immigrants: Labour Market Integration in Australia, Denmark, Germany and Sweden,* OECD Publishing, Paris.

OECD (2008), *International Migration Outlook: SOPEMI 2008,* OECD Publishing, Paris.

OECD (2008), *OECD Factbook 2008: Economic, Environmental and Social Statistics,* OECD Publishing, Paris.

OECD (2008), *Teaching, Learning and Assessment for Adults: Improving Foundation Skill,* OECD Publishing, Paris.

OECD (2009), *International Migration Outlook: SOPEMI 2009,* OECD Publishing, Paris.

Samuels, T. (2008), "The £7-Per-Hour Jobs Locals Don't Want", *www.bbcnews.com,* last updated 11 March.

Chapter 6

Adams, Jr. R.H. and J. Page (2005), "Do International Migration and Remittances Reduce Poverty in Developing Countries?" *Migration, Remittances and Development,* OECD Publishing, Paris.

Aglionby, J. and C. Moye (2007), "Distant Dream Homes", 10 November, *Financial Times,* London.

Benn, M. (2007), "International Development: Bringing it All Back Home", *Guardian Weekly,* 6 July, Guardian Newspapers Ltd., London.

Bilefsky, D. (2005) "Migration's Flip Side: One Big Empty Nest", 12 December, *The New York Times,* New York.

Cervantes, M. and D. Guellec (2002), "The Brain Drain: Old Myths, New Realities", May, *OECD Observer,* OECD, Paris.

Cohen, D. and M. Soto (2001), "Growth and Human Capital", *OECD Development Centre Working Papers,* No. 179, September, OECD Publishing, *http://dx.doi.org/10.1787/725160520154.*

Dayton-Johnson, J. *et al.* (2007), *Gaining from Migration: Towards a New Mobility System,* OECD Publishing, Paris.

DeParle, J. (2007), "Western Union Empire Moves Migrant Cash Home", 22 November, *The New York Times,* New York.

Dumont, J.-C., J.P. Martin and G. Spielvogel (2007), *Women on the Move: The Neglected Gender Dimension of the Brain Drain,* Discussion Paper No. 2,920, July, Institute for the Study of Labor (IZA), Bonn, *www.oecd.org/dataoecd/4/46/40232336.pdf.*

Ebrahim-zadeh, C. (2003), "Back to Basics", *Finance and Development,* March, No. 1, Vol. 40, International Monetary Fund, Washington DC.

Economist, The (2008), "A Turning Tide", 28 June, *The Economist,* The Economist Newspapers Ltd., London.

Fellahi, K. and S. de Lima (2005), "Western Union and the World Market For Remittances", *Migration, Remittances and Development,* OECD Publishing, Paris.

Fukada, T. (2008), "EPAs Clearing Way for Foreign Caregivers", 21 May, *The Japan Times,* The Japan Times Ltd., Tokyo.

Hennessy-Fiske, M. (2007), "Illegal Immigrants Wiring Money Have an Amigo: The Fed", 26 February, *Los Angeles Times,* Los Angeles, CA.

Lintner, B. (2003), "Flying Money", 2 October, *Far Eastern Economic Review,* Review Publishing Co., Hong Kong.

Mainichi Daily News (2008), "Diet to Open Door to Foreign Nurses, Care Workers", 18 April, *Mainichi Daily News,* The Mainichi Newspapers, Tokyo.

Martin, J.P. (2008), "Migration and the Global Economy: Some Stylised Facts", a paper from Directorate for Employment, Labour and Social Affairs, OECD, Paris, *www.oecd.org/dataoecd/27/54/40196342.pdf.*

Mullan, F. (2005), "The Metrics of the Physician Brain Drain", Vol. 353, No. 17, 27 October, *The New England Journal of Medicine,* Waltham, MA.

OECD (2004), *Trends in International Migration: SOPEMI 2003,* OECD Publishing, Paris.

OECD (2005), *Migration, Remittances and Development, The Development Dimension,* OECD Publishing, Paris.

OECD (2006), *International Migration Outlook: SOPEMI 2006,* OECD Publishing, Paris.

OECD (2007), *International Migration Outlook: SOPEMI 2007,* OECD Publishing, Paris.

OECD (2007), *Policy Coherence for Development 2007: Migration and Developing Countries,* OECD Publishing, Paris.

OECD (2007), *OECD Factbook 2007: Economic, Environmental and Social Statistics,* OECD Publishing, Paris.

OECD (2008), *International Migration Outlook: SOPEMI 2008,* OECD Publishing, Paris.

Office to Monitor and Combat Trafficking in Persons (2007), *Trafficking in Persons Report,* 12 June, US State Department, Washington DC.

Portes, A. (2007), "Migration, Development, and Segmented Assimilation: A Conceptual Review of the Evidence", Vol. 610, No. 1, *The Annals of the American Academy of Political and Social Science,* American Academy of Political and Social Science, Philadelphia, PA.

Sato, A. and A. Kobayashi (2008), "Indonesian Care Workers May Face Many Obstacles", 22 May, *The Daily Yomiuri,* Yomiuri Shimbun, Tokyo.

Straubharr, T. and F.P. Vădean (2005), "Introduction: International Migrant Remittances and their Role in Development", *Migration, Remittances and Development,* OECD Publishing, OECD, Paris.

World Bank (2008), *Migration and Remittances Factbook 2008, The International Bank for Development and Reconstruction/ TheWorld Bank,* Washington DC.

Chapter 7

Dayton-Johnson, J. *et al.* (2007), *Gaining from Migration: Towards a New Mobility System,* OECD Publishing, Paris.

García Zamora, R. (2005), "Collective Remittances and the 3x1 Program as a Transnational Social Learning Process", back-ground paper prepared for seminar on "Mexican Migrant Social and Civic Participation in the United States", 4-5 November, Woodrow Wilson International Centre for Scholars, Washington DC.

Gurría, A. (2008), Speech at the Launch of "A Profile of Immigrant Populations in the 21st Century", 20 February, *www.oecd.org/do cument/14/0,3343,en_2649_33931_40125838_1_1_1_1,00.html.*

Lemaître, G. (2005), "The Comparability of International Migration Statistics Problems and Prospects", *The Statistics Brief,* July, OECD, Paris.

Lemaître, G., *et al.* (2007), "Standardised Statistics on Immigrant Inflows: Results, Sources and Methods", a paper produced by the Directorate for Employment, Labour and Social Affairs, OECD, Paris, *www.oecd.org/dataoecd/39/29/38832099.pdf.*

McGee, H. and C. Brennan (2008), "Ahern Says Integration 'Huge' Issue", 24 April, *The Irish Times,* Dublin.

OECD (2007), *International Migration Outlook: SOPEMI 2007,* OECD Publishing, Paris.

OECD (2008), *International Migration Outlook: SOPEMI 2008,* OECD Publishing, Paris.

OECD (2008), *A Profile of Immigrant Populations in the 21st Century: Data from OECD Countries,* OECD Publishing, Paris.

OECD (2008), *OECD Economic Surveys: Ireland,* OECD Publishing, Paris.

Ratha, D., S. Mohapatra and Z. Xu (2008), *Migration and Development Brief,* 11 November, World Bank, Washington DC.

World Bank, The (2008), *Migration and Remittances Factbook 2008,* The International Bank for Reconstruction and Development/ The World Bank, Washington DC.

Photos credits:

Cover illustration: © Baloncici/Fotolia.com.

Images: pp. 8-9: © pictu-resbyrob/Alamy;

pp. 18-19 © 2008 JupiterImages Corporation;

pp. 40-41 © Hollingsworth/Photodisc/Getty Images;

pp. 62-63 © Tom Grill/Corbis;

pp. 84-85 © Photoalto/Inmagine;

pp. 110-111 © OECD;

pp. 134-135 © Inmagine ltd.